EVALUATION OF
QUANTIFICATION OF MARGINS AND UNCERTAINTIES
METHODOLOGY FOR ASSESSING AND CERTIFYING THE RELIABILITY OF THE NUCLEAR STOCKPILE

Committee on the Evaluation of Quantification of Margins and Uncertainties Methodology for Assessing and Certifying the Reliability of the Nuclear Stockpile

Division on Engineering and Physical Sciences

NATIONAL RESEARCH COUNCIL
OF THE NATIONAL ACADEMIES

THE NATIONAL ACADEMIES PRESS
Washington, D.C.
www.nap.edu

THE NATIONAL ACADEMIES PRESS   500 Fifth Street, N.W.   Washington, DC 20001

NOTICE: The project that is the subject of this report was approved by the Governing Board of the National Research Council, whose members are drawn from the councils of the National Academy of Sciences, the National Academy of Engineering, and the Institute of Medicine. The members of the committee responsible for the report were chosen for their special competences and with regard for appropriate balance.

This project was supported by Contract No. DE-AT01-07NA78285 between the National Academy of Sciences and the U.S. Department of Energy. Any opinions, findings, conclusions, or recommendations expressed in this publication are those of the author(s) and do not necessarily reflect the view of the organizations or agencies that provided support for this project.

International Standard Book Number-13: 978-0-309-12853-7
International Standard Book Number-10: 0-309-12853-6

Copies of the unclassified version of this report are available from

The National Academies Press
500 Fifth Street, N.W.
Box 285
Washington, DC 20055

800-624-6242
202-334-3313 (in the Washington metropolitan area)
Internet http://www.nap.edu

Copyright 2009 by the National Academy of Sciences. All rights reserved.

Printed in the United States of America

THE NATIONAL ACADEMIES
Advisers to the Nation on Science, Engineering, and Medicine

The **National Academy of Sciences** is a private, nonprofit, self-perpetuating society of distinguished scholars engaged in scientific and engineering research, dedicated to the furtherance of science and technology and to their use for the general welfare. Upon the authority of the charter granted to it by the Congress in 1863, the Academy has a mandate that requires it to advise the federal government on scientific and technical matters. Dr. Ralph J. Cicerone is president of the National Academy of Sciences.

The **National Academy of Engineering** was established in 1964, under the charter of the National Academy of Sciences, as a parallel organization of outstanding engineers. It is autonomous in its administration and in the selection of its members, sharing with the National Academy of Sciences the responsibility for advising the federal government. The National Academy of Engineering also sponsors engineering programs aimed at meeting national needs, encourages education and research, and recognizes the superior achievements of engineers. Dr. Charles M. Vest is president of the National Academy of Engineering.

The **Institute of Medicine** was established in 1970 by the National Academy of Sciences to secure the services of eminent members of appropriate professions in the examination of policy matters pertaining to the health of the public. The Institute acts under the responsibility given to the National Academy of Sciences by its congressional charter to be an adviser to the federal government and, upon its own initiative, to identify issues of medical care, research, and education. Dr. Harvey V. Fineberg is president of the Institute of Medicine.

The **National Research Council** was organized by the National Academy of Sciences in 1916 to associate the broad community of science and technology with the Academy's purposes of furthering knowledge and advising the federal government. Functioning in accordance with general policies determined by the Academy, the Council has become the principal operating agency of both the National Academy of Sciences and the National Academy of Engineering in providing services to the government, the public, and the scientific and engineering communities. The Council is administered jointly by both Academies and the Institute of Medicine. Dr. Ralph J. Cicerone and Dr. Charles M. Vest are chair and vice chair, respectively, of the National Research Council.

www.national-academies.org

COMMITTEE ON EVALUATION OF QUANTIFICATION OF MARGINS AND UNCERTAINTIES METHODOLOGY FOR ASSESSING AND CERTIFYING THE RELIABILITY OF THE NUCLEAR STOCKPILE

JOHN F. AHEARNE (NAE), Sigma Xi, The Scientific Research Society, *Chair*
MARVIN ADAMS, Texas A&M University
JOHN CORNWALL, University of California, Los Angeles
DOUGLAS EARDLEY, University of California, Santa Barbara
B. JOHN GARRICK (NAE), Independent Consultant
RICHARD L. GARWIN (NAS/NAE/IOM), IBM Thomas J. Watson Research Center (fellow emeritus)
SYDELL P. GOLD,[1] Independent Consultant
YOGENDRA GUPTA, Washington State University
DAVID HAMMER, Cornell University
THEODORE HARDEBECK, Science Applications International Corporation
JOHN KAMMERDIENER, Independent Consultant
SALLIE KELLER-McNULTY, Rice University
ERNEST J. MONIZ, Massachusetts Institute of Technology
MICHAEL ORTIZ, California Institute of Technology
JERRY PAUL, University of Tennessee
ROBERT ROSNER, Argonne National Laboratory
ROBERT SELDEN, Independent Consultant

Staff

RICHARD ROWBERG, Study Director
GREG EYRING, Senior Program Officer, Air Force Science Board
MICAH LOWENTHAL, Senior Program Officer, Nuclear and Radiation Studies Board
KEVIN CROWLEY, Board Director, Nuclear and Radiation Studies Board
MARGARET MARSH HUYNH, Senior Program Assistant, Computer Science and Telecommunications Board (to September 2007)
JANICE SABUDA, Senior Program Assistant, Computer Science and Telecommunications Board (September 2007 to March 2008)

---

[1]Deceased, March 4, 2008.

RADHIKA CHARI, Administrative Coordinator, Computer Science and
 Telecommunications Board (March 2008 to April 2008)
ERIC WHITAKER, Senior Program Assistant, Computer Science and
 Telecommunications Board (April 2008 to present)

Preface

Maintaining the capabilities of the nuclear weapons stockpile and performing the annual assessment for the stockpile's certification involves a wide range of processes, technologies, and expertise. An important and valuable element helping to link those components is the quantification of margins and uncertainties (QMU) framework. In 2006, Congress asked the National Research Council to evaluate the QMU methodology as used by the national security laboratories. The National Nuclear Security Administration (NNSA) of the U.S. Department of Energy (DOE) then affirmed its interest in this request. Congress and NNSA were interested in how the national security labs were using QMU, how it was being used for the annual assessment, whether there were problematic differences among the three national security labs in the way they were applying QMU, and whether QMU could be used to help certify a proposed reliable replacement warhead. This report presents an assessment of each of these four issues and includes findings and recommendations to help guide laboratory and NNSA implementation and development of the QMU framework and congressional oversight of those activities.

At several places in the report, reference is made to an Annex that contains classified information. The Annex includes information the U.S. Department of Energy and the National Academy of Sciences have determined is not releasable to the public because it would disclose matters described in title 5 U.S.C. Section 552(b).

Acknowledgments

This report has been reviewed in draft form by individuals chosen for their diverse perspectives and technical expertise, in accordance with procedures approved by the NRC's Report Review Committee. The purpose of this independent review is to provide candid and critical comments that will assist the institution in making its published report as sound as possible and to ensure that the report meets institutional standards for objectivity, evidence, and responsiveness to the study charge. The review comments and draft manuscript remain confidential to protect the integrity of the deliberative process. We wish to thank the following individuals for their review of this report:

Will Happer (NAS), Princeton University,
Jon Helton, Arizona State University (retired),
Raymond Jeanloz (NAS), University of California, Berkeley,
ADM Richard Mies, U.S. Navy (retired),
William Press (NAS), University of Texas at Austin
Richard Wagner, Lawrence Livermore National Laboratory (retired), and
Ellen Williams (NAS), University of Maryland.

Although the reviewers listed above have provided many constructive comments and suggestions, they were not asked to endorse the conclusions or recommendations, nor did they see the final draft of the report before its release. The review of this report was overseen by Chris G.

Whipple (NAE), ENVIRON. Appointed by the National Research Council, he was responsible for making certain that an independent examination of this report was carried out in accordance with institutional procedures and that all review comments were carefully considered. Responsibility for the final content of this report rests entirely with the authoring committee and the institution.

Contents

SUMMARY 1

1 OVERVIEW 4
   Introduction, 4
      Context, 4
      Issues, 6
      Statement of Task, 7
   Background, 9
      Definition and Current Implementation of QMU, 9
      Study Process, 16

2 USE OF THE QMU METHODOLOGY (TASK 1) 18
   Uncertainty Quantification, 20
   Uncertainty Propagation and Aggregation, 21
   Sources of Uncertainty, 23
   Representation of a Simple Performance Gate, 25
   Introducing More Complex Probability Distributions, 26
   Direct Computation of Distribution Overlap, 28
   Phenomenology of Nuclear Explosions, 30
   Role of Modeling and Simulation in QMU, 31

3 QMU AND THE ANNUAL ASSESSMENT 34
   REVIEW (TASK 2)
   Sandia National Laboratories, 35

Los Alamos National Laboratory, 36
Lawrence Livermore National Laboratory, 36
Performance Gates, 37
Peer Review Opportunities, 37

4 COMPARISON AND CONTRAST OF THE USE   39
  OF QMU (TASK 3)

5 QMU AND THE RRW PROGRAM (TASK 4)   43

APPENDIXES

A A Probabilistic Risk Assessment Perspective of QMU   51
B Committee Biographical Information   67
C Glossary   77

Summary

BACKGROUND

In order to meet their obligation to help maintain the capabilities of the nuclear weapons stockpile and to perform the annual assessment for the stockpile's certification, the national security laboratories—Los Alamos National Laboratory (LANL), Lawrence Livermore National Laboratory (LLNL), and Sandia National Laboratories (SNL)—of the National Nuclear Security Administration (NNSA) employ a wide range of processes, technologies, and expertise. The quantification of margins and uncertainties (QMU) framework plays a key role in helping to link those three elements. While it does not replace existing assessment methodologies, QMU makes a number of critical contributions. Concerns about its use, however, led the Congress to ask the National Research Council to evaluate (1) how the national security labs were using QMU, including any significant differences among the three labs; (2) its use in the annual assessment; and (3) whether the application of QMU to assess the proposed reliable replacement warhead (RRW) could reduce the likelihood of resuming underground nuclear testing.[1] This request was endorsed by the NNSA.

---

[1]Throughout this report, the terms nuclear test and nuclear testing refer to nuclear explosions.

MAJOR FINDINGS AND RECOMMENDATIONS

QMU is a sound and valuable framework that helps the national security laboratories carry out the Department of Energy's (DOE) responsibility to maintain the nation's nuclear weapons capabilities. Its value is evident in many ways, including for the organization of the many stockpile stewardship tools such as the advanced simulation and computing codes and computing and for the allocation of important resources. The national security laboratories and NNSA should expand their use of QMU while continuing to develop, improve, and increase application of the methodology. While they have focused much attention on uncertainty quantification, a broader effort is needed in this area, including further development of the methodology to identify, aggregate, and propagate uncertainties. In a related issue, the identification of performance gates (see Glossary) and their margins is incomplete.

QMU also relies on expert judgment, and effective implementation of QMU will depend on maintaining a quality staff at the national security labs, particularly weapons designers. Finally, the national security labs are not taking full advantage of their own probabilistic risk assessment capabilities. Several probabilistic risk assessment concepts could be applied to QMU applications. In particular, the national security labs should investigate the probability of frequency (see Glossary) approach in presenting uncertainties.

The application of QMU in the annual assessment review conducted by the national security laboratories is growing and providing important insights, such as a basis for confidence in stockpile performance. Its use in the review is still limited, however, and should be expanded. In particular, margins (M) and uncertainties (U) should be reported for all gates that are judged to be critical for warhead performance.

While there are differences among the national security labs in how the QMU methodology is implemented, these differences can enhance the development of QMU. Different approaches for estimating uncertainties, for example, should continue to be explored. Differences in definitions and terminology, however, can inhibit communication and transparency, and the national security labs should agree upon a common set of definitions and terms. Consistency and transparency of the application of QMU are also being inhibited by the lack of documentation. Both NNSA and the labs should issue QMU guidance documents in time for the current assessment cycle.

QMU can be used to evaluate new warheads, such as the RRW design, and for certification. If the design of a new nuclear warhead is sufficiently "close" to existing tested designs, the new warhead could, in principle, be certified without nuclear tests, based on archival tests, modeling and simulation tools, and a more mature QMU methodology. The design labs (LANL and LLNL) should provide detailed justification for use of archival tests to support any proposed RRW design and investigate ways to help quantify "closeness." Also essential for a credible RRW certification process are expanded peer review, documentation, and experimentation without nuclear testing.

1

Overview

INTRODUCTION

Context

When the moratorium on nuclear testing went into effect in 1992, the Department of Energy (DOE) began to develop other ways to maintain the nation's nuclear weapons stockpile. In 1993, Congress and the President directed DOE to "establish a stewardship program to ensure the preservation of the core intellectual and technical competencies of the United States in nuclear weapons."[1] The Stockpile Stewardship Program's (SSP's) objective was to develop ways to simulate—with computer models and experiments that remain subcritical—the various processes that take place during a nuclear weapon explosion and to apply the knowledge gained to extend the life of the existing weapons in the stockpile. The SSP evolved over time, and in 1999, DOE created 18 subprograms—called campaigns—to organize the science and stockpile maintenance activities.[2] The objective of these campaigns has been to develop the critical capabilities for assessing the performance, safety and reliability of the stockpile without the need for nuclear testing. Finally, in 2000, Congress

---

[1] U.S. Congress, The National Defense Authorization Act for Fiscal Year 1994, P.L. 103-160, Sec. 3135 (1994).
[2] U.S. Government Accountability Office, NNSA Needs to Refine and More Effectively Manage Its New Approach for Assessing and Certifying Nuclear Weapons. GAO-06-261 (2006).

created a new, separate entity within DOE—the National Nuclear Security Administration (NNSA)—whose primary task is to maintain the nuclear weapons stockpile.

Every year, the SSP must assess the safety, reliability, performance, and effectiveness of the nuclear weapons stockpile in the absence of nuclear testing. The directors of the three national security laboratories—Los Alamos National Laboratory (LANL), Lawrence Livermore National Laboratory (LLNL), and Sandia National Laboratories (SNL)—are required to submit letters each year to the Secretary of Energy with their assessment of whether the stockpile is safe, reliable, and effective and expressing their opinions on whether nuclear testing needs to be resumed in the subsequent year to assure those conditions.

In 2001, the three national security labs began using a framework called quantification of margins and uncertainties (QMU) to help with the assessment process. QMU is a decision-support framework that provides a means for quantifying the laboratories' confidence that the critical stages of a nuclear weapon will operate as intended. In general terms, its purpose is to provide a systematic means to apply—using sophisticated simulation models—the varied output of the science base of the SSP to the assessment of the nuclear weapons stockpile. This output includes the aboveground nonnuclear and subcritical experiments, data from past underground nuclear tests, and expert judgments of the weapons scientists.

QMU is an important part of the assessment process and one that is growing in significance. It is also used to help set priorities for SSP research and engineering activities. And it helps to identify those components or operating characteristics of the various nuclear weapons in the stockpile that put them most at risk.

Recently, the NNSA reported that extending the life of the existing stockpile would become increasingly difficult over time.[3,4] It has raised concerns about how the need for continual refurbishments of existing warheads could affect the reliability of the stockpile. Over time, it argued, there would be a buildup of small changes that would cause the warhead to become more and more removed from the tested design.[5] To counter

---

[3]U.S. Congress, Congressional Research Service, The Reliable Replacement Warhead Program: Background and Current Developments, RL32929 (updated November 8, 2007), p. 1.

[4]This concern relates not so much to replacement of control systems and electronics that can be fully tested but more to the nuclear explosive package itself. Thus, the nuclear explosive package is the primary target of the QMU process. It is important to clearly document changes already made or expected to be made to the nuclear explosive package that would result in the warhead becoming more and more removed from the tested design.

[5]U.S. Congress, Testimony by NNSA Acting Administrator Thomas D'Agostino before the House Armed Services Committee, March 20, 2007.

this trend, NNSA proposed a major restructuring of the nuclear weapons program including the development of a warhead[6] class or type known as the reliable replacement warhead (RRW). The aim of the RRW program is to develop a warhead based on existing warheads whose performance, safety, security, and manufacturability could be assured with high confidence and whose stewardship, without the need for nuclear testing, would be relatively straightforward for decades to come. Even though it would be based on tested weapons, however, the RRW would not be identical to any existing weapon. NNSA is requiring the use of the QMU methodology as an important—but not the only—component of the certification process for the RRW. As a first step, a competition for the first RRW design was held in 2007 between LANL-SNL and LLNL-SNL, and NNSA selected the latter's design.

Issues

The QMU framework is becoming an increasingly important part of the nuclear weapons assessment process, and the national security laboratories and NNSA express optimism about its future value to the SSP. Nevertheless, QMU is a relatively new component of the program, and both internal and external reviews over the past few years have raised issues about the QMU framework and its application to nuclear weapons assessment.[7] As a consequence, both Congress and the NNSA expressed interest in late 2006 in further evaluation of the QMU framework and its application. Some of the issues driving this interest are the role of expert judgment; the difficulties in quantifying margins and uncertainties for complex systems; the variable quality and quantity of test data that are needed to validate warhead simulation codes that are used to develop good quantitative estimates of margins and uncertainties; and how to properly incorporate statistical considerations into those estimates. It should be noted that these issues would probably arise with any approach to assessment and certification and are not unique to the QMU methodology. Furthermore, the QMU framework can be expected to evolve as new tools and methodologies become available.

One review also expressed concern about the current implementation practices of the QMU methodology.[8] According to this analysis, there

---

[6]The term warhead encompasses both missile systems and gravity bombs.

[7]Review by the Government Accountability Office; JASON, Quantification of Margins and Uncertainties (QMU), JSR-04-330, Mitre Corporation (March 2005); U.S. Department of Defense, Report on the Friendly Reviews of QMU at the NNSA Laboratories, Defense Program Science Council (March 2004); Raymond Orbach, Undersecretary of Energy for Science, Presentation to the committee, October 26, 2007.

[8]Review by the Government Accountability Office.

might be important differences between LLNL and LANL in the application of QMU and between the two design laboratories and SNL in the application of QMU.[9]

These issues are of particular interest to Congress in connection with the proposed RRW. If this warhead is to be developed without nuclear testing, an assessment that involves application of a QMU framework as a key component of the certification process appears critical.[10] As with assessment of the existing stockpile, however, the other key elements of the weapons program—the underground nuclear test data archive, expert judgment, aboveground experiments, simulation models, and so on—will contribute to the assessment and certification of the RRW in ways other than as input to the implementation of the QMU framework. Nevertheless, dependence on the QMU methodology appears to be growing, leading to increased congressional interest in this aspect of the weapons program.

Statement of Task

In 2006, as a result of congressional concerns about the methodology, implementation, and likely role of QMU in any potential RRW, the House Armed Services Committee inserted language in HR 5122, the John Warner National Defense Authorization Act for Fiscal Year 2007, requesting the National Academy of Sciences to conduct an independent evaluation of the QMU methodology employed by the national security laboratories and to say whether this methodology could be used to certify an RRW without underground nuclear testing. The Senate agreed to nearly identical language in the conference report for the bill, and the request was enacted into law in the National Defense Authorization Act of FY2007, P.L. 109-364, Sec. 3. The request was independently endorsed by NNSA, which added a task to be covered in a second phase of the study.

For the purposes of this report, the Congress and DOE requested that the National Academy of Sciences carry out the following tasks:

- (1) Evaluate the use of the quantification of margins and uncertainties methodology by the national security laboratories, including underlying assumptions of weapons performance, the ability of modeling and simulation tools to predict nuclear explosive

---

[9]SNL also uses QMU as part of its assessment and stewardship activities. Because SNL focuses on the engineering aspects of nuclear weapons, however, there are some differences in the way it applies QMU.

[10]JASON, Reliable Replacement Warhead Executive Summary, JSR-07-336E, Mitre Corporation (September 2007), p. 7.

package characteristics, and the recently proposed modifications to that methodology to calculate margins and uncertainties.
- (2) Evaluate the manner in which that methodology is used to conduct the annual assessments of the nuclear weapons stockpile.
- (3) Evaluate how the use of that methodology compares and contrasts between the national security laboratories.
- (4) Evaluate whether the application of the quantification of margins and uncertainties used for annual assessments and certification of the nuclear weapons stockpile can be applied to the planned Reliable Replacement Warhead program so as to carry out the objective of that program to reduce the likelihood of the resumption of underground testing of nuclear weapons.
- (5) Assess how archived data are used in the evaluation of margins and uncertainties. This includes use for baselining codes, informing annual assessment, assessing significant finding investigations (SFIs), etc. Are the design labs fully exploiting the data for QMU? Are they missing opportunities?

Tasks 1 through 4 are covered in this report. A second report will cover Task 5.

Some other recent congressional actions concerning the nation's nuclear weapons program are also worth noting. In the FY2008 Consolidated Appropriations Act, Congress denied funding for the RRW program and provided new funding for advanced certification.[11] In accompanying language, Congress stated that before any such warhead was developed, "a new strategic nuclear deterrent mission assessment for the 21st century is required to define the associated stockpile requirements and determine the scope of the weapons complex modernization plans." Accordingly, it directed NNSA "to develop and submit to the Congress a comprehensive nuclear weapons strategy for the 21st century." In conjunction with this strategic planning effort, Congress also requested that NNSA "develop a long-term scientific capability roadmap for the national laboratories." In the same legislation, Congress directed NNSA to begin a new Science Campaign called Advanced Certification to address "significant systemic gaps in NNSA's stockpile certification process" and funded this effort at $15 million.

In the conference report accompanying the FY2008 Defense Authorization Bill, Congress urged NNSA "to approach the RRW program cautiously, with a commitment to address and resolve all issues as completely

---

[11]U.S. Congress, Consolidated Appropriations Act, 2008, Division C—Energy and Water Development and Related Agencies Appropriations Act, 2008, House Appropriations Committee Print to accompany P.L. 110-161 (2008), p. 583.

as possible."[12] The authorization bill also called for an examination of U.S. nuclear policy and strategic posture.

BACKGROUND

Definition and Current Implementation of QMU

This section provides a description of how the QMU methodology is currently being implemented. As was noted above, QMU is an important part of the process by which nuclear weapons computer simulation models, experiments producing no nuclear yield, prior underground nuclear tests, and expert judgment are brought to bear to assess the reliability of the existing weapons stockpile. The QMU process is analogous to the concept of engineering safety margins—that is, a system is designed so that its operating margins are far enough removed from the failure thresholds to instill high confidence that the system will work reliably even though the magnitude and uncertainty of the margin for a particular performance metric (for example, the voltage applied to a detonator—see Figure 1-1) may not be known with great precision. It is important to note that the QMU framework is not the only process underpinning such an assessment. This comparison of margins and uncertainties leaves out many important features and nuances. The QMU framework is discussed in greater detail in Box 1-1.

It might be helpful to consider the following example using QMU to assess the function of one of the unclassified performance gates in a typical nuclear explosive. A voltage must be applied to a detonator in order for it to function properly. Figure 1-1 provides a graphical representation of the process. The graph is called a cliff chart because the performance curve has the form of a cliff at the threshold of operation. Let us assume that it has been determined experimentally that 100 volts (V) is required for the detonator to operate. This is the threshold value, $V_{T,BE}$, in Figure 1-1. Also assume that the test of many detonators of the type used shows that the required voltage varies by no more than 5 V. This uncertainty in the threshold voltage is given by U_2 in Figure 1-1. The engineers therefore design a firing system that applies 150 V with a maximum variation of 10 V. The latter is the uncertainty in the firing system voltage at its design point, U_1, in Figure 1-1. The QMU analysis states that the margin, M, is 50 V (150 V − 100 V) and the total uncertainty, U, equals 10 V (U_1, the uncertainty in the applied voltage) + 5 V (U_2, the uncertainty in the firing voltage) = 15 V. Consequently, M/U = 50 V/15 V = 3.3, which is

---

[12]U.S. Congress, H. Report 110-477 (2007), p. 1323.

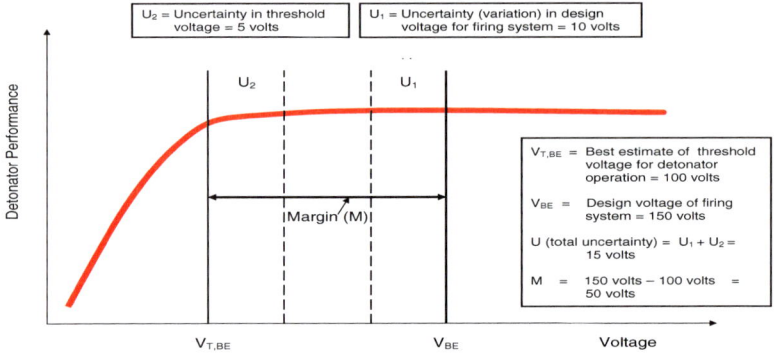

FIGURE 1-1 Cliff chart representation of detonator performance.

**Box 1-1
QMU**

QMU is a framework that utilizes data and analysis from many experimental and computational sources to help assess the performance of nuclear weapons. One purpose of this framework is to provide a transparent, systematic approach by which designers and the national security laboratories can do two things:

- Quantify their confidence in the performance and reliability of a weapon design through a set of high-level metrics, such as the ratio of a performance margin, M, to the uncertainties of important weapon subsystems.
- Communicate this confidence clearly to people outside the design community, including government officials and the general public.

The scientific and mathematical methodologies included in the QMU framework have been applied by the laboratories to evaluate both the yield margin for a primary to drive a secondary and a related overall uncertainty.

However, it should not be thought that the construction of a single overall margin and overall uncertainty is the essence of how the labs implement QMU. The QMU framework and its many experimental, analytic, and computational resources are also applied to many weapons subsystems and subelements in ways most appropriate to them, with the quantification of margins and uncertainties for each. Ultimately these many margins and uncertainties are combined in assessing the entire nuclear explosive package. QMU has been used for today's nuclear weapons and their predecessors as well as for the RRW design.

QMU provides input for a risk-informed decision-making process that combines quantitative analysis and expert judgment and requires answers to the following questions:

- What are the key gates through which a weapon's performance must pass in order to meet its design objectives? Can a necessary and sufficient set be identified?
- What are the key metrics for each gate, and what are the thresholds for each metric?

- If a gate is passed with only a narrow margin, how does this affect the thresholds of other gates?
- What are the best and most reliable tools for quantifying or (when precise quantification is unnecessary) bounding technical and scientific uncertainty?
- What are the most important scientific and engineering uncertainties?
- How much is enough? That is, how much understanding of a particular basic science or engineering issue is needed? How small must an uncertainty be made, consistent with achieving confidence required for weapons performance, reliability, and surety?
- What is the uncertainty budget (or goal) for the system or subsystem under consideration?
- How are subsystem uncertainties being aggregated into a bound or quantification of overall system uncertainty?
- What joint computational and experimental activities are needed?

One fundamental scientific tool is the estimation of uncertainties with sensitivity analyses, as applied to or backed up by an assessment of failure modes, cliffs, margins, mining the data from underground nuclear tests, and experimental validation.

The fundamental output of QMU is a measure, common to the three national security laboratories, of confidence in the performance of specific systems or subsystems as quantified in a comparison of margins, M, and uncertainties, U, in a credible and transparent form that is easy to convey to others.

A valid assessment and certification QMU methodology has five essential criteria. It must be (1) complete, (2) connected, (3) validated, (4) demonstrated, and (5) communicated.

The *completeness* aspects of QMU can benefit from the structured methodology and discipline of quantitative risk assessment and probabilistic risk assessment. Construction of a functional sequence also allows experts of all varieties to weigh in on the problem. An ideal QMU methodology is not complete until all failure modes are identified and incorporated. Transparency is important here.

A QMU methodology is *connected* if the interactions between failure modes are included. Application of QMU to only a single failure mode provides no connections. It is not enough to calculate a valid margin and uncertainty for each failure mode. The functional interconnection of modes must be included. For instance, if one failure mode passes near its minimum (or maximum) it can affect the nominal performance of subsequent failure modes. The convolution and propagation of uncertainties is almost certainly an important part of QMU. The evaluation of the stockpile sequence must be connected to the deployment and use sequence. Changes and differences in the stockpiled warheads do affect both the reliability and performance of the nuclear explosive package.

A QMU methodology should be *validated* and verified in much the same way as a simulation. *Demonstration* is the key to transparency and acceptance of a QMU methodology. QMU must be applied to a real example. Demonstration is the strongest form of definition. The obvious example is the RRW. A demonstration of RRW certification will show that a relaxation of the requirements of size, weight, and limited quantities of key materials can allow the designer to increase margins. Increased margins can overcome possible increases in uncertainty for each of the failure nodes. In the final analysis the values of M and U are important but much more is required for an assessment or certification.

Finally, the QMU methodology must be *communicated* to the community of interested parties (labs, DOE, DOD, and Congress).

the measure of confidence that the detonator will work as designed. A similar procedure is applied to the other performance gates that perform in a serial or serial/parallel fashion. It should be emphasized that in this simple example, the uncertainties can be added. In a more complex system, the uncertainties might be statistical in nature and such a simple aggregation might not be valid. Also, the computation of the margin and uncertainties did not require sophisticated computational models, which would be needed for more complex systems.

For application to nuclear weapons, the centerpiece of the QMU methodology is the set of complex weapons simulation codes that have been developed over the last 65 years. These codes are made up of many physical models describing weapons physics, data from prior underground nonnuclear and nuclear tests, data from subcritical and aboveground experiments, expert judgment, and properties of materials (equations of state, opacity, nuclear reaction cross sections, etc.). Adjustments are made to various inputs and model parameters in the simulation to match analytic calculations and selected test data.

The first step in the QMU methodology is to identify the critical performance gates. The term "performance gate" will be used throughout the report to represent performance indicators, checkpoints, thresholds, etc. As such, a performance gate is represented by a range of acceptable values, defined by subsystem margins and uncertainties, for the performance of each of many subsystems in the chain of events occurring in a nuclear explosion. Performance gates are associated with the key components and operating characteristics of the weapon whose failure would severely compromise the overall performance of the weapon. The performance of these components and their characteristics are described by metrics (quantitative measures) determined by experimental data and computer simulations. A metric can be any quantity that depends on the physical characteristics and state of the system and/or its operation. Performance gates test cliffs (thresholds), quantities, configurations, and coincidences. They are "high-level indicators of some aspect of the system's operation."[13] For simplicity, only cliffs are addressed in this section. An example is the energy of the imploding plutonium (Pu) pit. The system can be represented by performance gates through which or cliffs over which the metric must "pass" for successful operation. A nuclear warhead is so complex that it is not easy to devise a quick and readily understood way of presenting information about performance gates, metrics, margins, and uncertainties. This is one of the important tasks for the QMU framework.

---

[13]D.H. Sharp and M.M. Wood-Schultz, QMU and Nuclear Weapons Certification: What's Under the Hood? *Los Alamos Science* 28 (2003): 48.

OVERVIEW

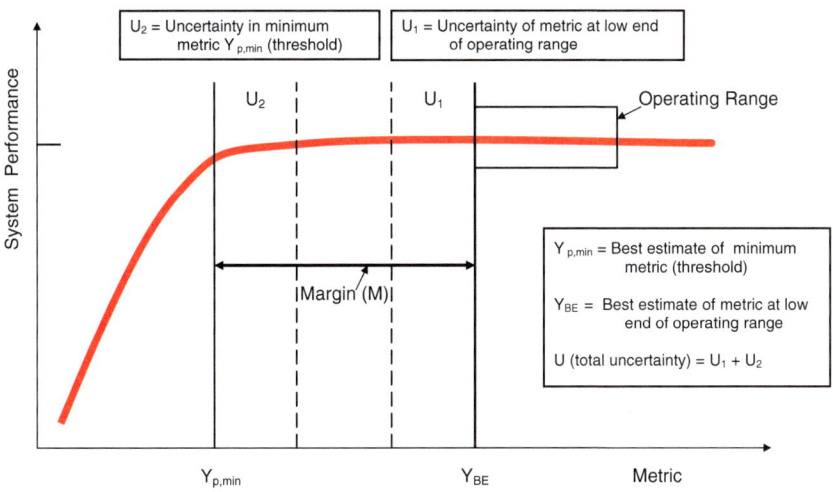

FIGURE 1-2 Cliff chart representation of system performance.

One way of presenting results is to use the cliff chart graphical representation introduced above. Figure 1-2 shows a generalized cliff chart. This graphic predated QMU itself and it is still being used for QMU purposes. The cliff chart is a high-level summary and displays the expected system performance as a function of some metric (such as primary yield), with margins and uncertainties in that metric indicated by a simple band of values. Underlying this graphic are the detailed calculations called for by the QMU framework; they deal with a large number of metrics not explicitly indicated on the cliff chart. Generally, these metrics—including those shown explicitly on a cliff chart—are described by probability distribution functions, not by a simple band of values. There is a minimum value—threshold—that each metric must meet or exceed for the component or characteristic to operate properly. For example, the criticality of Pu in the weapon's primary must reach a threshold value for the primary to produce sufficient yield. The amount by which a minimum expected metric exceeds this threshold value is the operating margin, M, for that component or characteristic. In normally functioning weapons, where all key metrics are operating above this margin, the system performance would be in the design range. The codes, along with underground nuclear test data, expert judgment, and aboveground experiments,[14] are used to estimate the threshold and lowest expected performance level and, accordingly, the value of the margin for each component or operating

---

[14] Aboveground experiments are by definition subcritical (see Glossary).

characteristic. The cliff chart represents only a summary of what is done in the QMU methodology and must not be confused with the framework itself or with the huge amounts of data and simulations that back up the cliff chart.

The most difficult part of using the QMU framework for evaluating nuclear weapons performance is identifying, characterizing, quantifying, and aggregating the large number of uncertainties, U, that arise. There are uncertainties in the simulation codes' predicted threshold value and the operating range lower boundary of the margin at each stage of the warhead process. (These are given by U_2 and U_1, respectively, in Figure 1-2.) One class of uncertainties is called epistemic or systematic uncertainties; it includes incomplete knowledge of the parameters describing the phenomena of interest, incorrect and missing physics models, approximations and numerical errors, code bugs, and the like. In principle these can be lessened by gathering more knowledge and data. A second class of uncertainties—random or aleatory uncertainties—is intrinsic; it includes manufacturing variability, variability in materials used, and test-to-test variability.[15]

The total uncertainty for a performance gate is the sum of the threshold uncertainty and the minimum performance uncertainty. If the uncertainties are large enough, they will erode or destroy confidence that the component or operating characteristic will perform as designed. Therefore, a condition of reliable operation is that the margin must be larger than the total uncertainty found by aggregating all the subsystem uncertainties. This is expressed as a confidence ratio, M/U. If M/U $\gg$ 1, the degree of confidence that the system will perform as expected should be high. If M/U is not significantly greater than 1, the system needs careful examination. (This would be even more true if M/U $\leq$ 1.) Obviously, it is important to understand M, U, and M/U to be able to specify confidence levels with these quantities.

Spreads of uncertainties in output values of different performance gates caused by uncertain input parameters are estimated by performing sensitivity analyses[16] across the plausible ranges of input parameters, with a large number of runs of the simulation codes, each with different param-

---

[15]See, for example, G.W. Parry and P.W. Winter, Characterization and Evaluation of Uncertainty in Probabilistic Risk Analysis, *Nuclear Safety* 22(1) (1981): 28-42; M.E. Paté-Cornell, Uncertainties in Risk Analysis: Six Levels of Treatment, *Reliability Engineering and System Safety* 54(2-3) (1996): 95-111; and J.C. Helton, Uncertainty and Sensitivity Analysis in the Presence of Stochastic and Subjective Uncertainty, *Journal of Statistical Computation and Simulation* 57(1-4) (1997): 3-76.

[16]See, for example, A. Saltelli, K.P.-S. Chan, and E.M. Scott, eds., *Sensitivity Analysis*, New York, N.Y.: Wiley (2000); A. Saltelli, S. Tarantola, and K.P.-S. Chan, A Quantitative Model-Independent Method for Global Sensitivity Analysis of Model Output, *Technometrics* 41(1)

eter settings intended to explore this plausible range. These computed code sensitivities are often assumed to be representative of sensitivities in the physical systems being modeled. To the extent possible, the outputs of the computer models are validated by comparing them to experimental data—primarily from archived underground nuclear test data and aboveground experiments—in an effort to estimate uncertainties arising from gaps and errors in the physics models. These comparisons can lead to enhancements of the models, improving their predictive capabilities. Uncertainty is further increased, however, by the fact that underground nuclear test experiments were only rarely conducted at performance thresholds, and data from aboveground experiments extend over a very limited range of the performance space of a nuclear explosion.

The codes themselves are sources of uncertainty. At least three of these sources of uncertainty must be addressed. The models must be verified to eliminate bugs and to control numerical errors so that the adopted physical models are correctly solved. The models also must be validated by experiments so that the simulation is a faithful representation of the processes it is intended to emulate. And the conceptual design must be correct so that all the essential features of the overall performance have been accurately included in the simulation. (More information on this topic is included in Note 10 in the classified Annex.)

An important aspect of uncertainty quantification is to calculate the (output) probability distribution of a given metric and from that distribution to estimate the uncertainty of that metric. The meaning of the confidence ratio (M/U) depends significantly on this definition and on the way subsystem uncertainties are aggregated to an overall system uncertainty. Knowing this distribution allows determining the degree to which the threshold and operating range uncertainties might overlap and, therefore, the likelihood that the M/U ratio is not defined.

Sensitivity analyses are one part of the process of transforming initial (input) uncertainties into final (output) uncertainties. It may happen that a particular bit of input knowledge is poorly known—for example, some property of some material. But sensitivity analysis may reveal that the actual value of that property has little effect on the final output when uncertainties from all sources are aggregated into a system uncertainty. It may also happen that there is no particular input information on the probability distribution function (PDF) of certain quantities, in which case analysts begin with a simple spread of plausible values for that quantity. Sensitivity analyses, however, will help provide information about the output uncertainty for that quantity.

(1999): 39-56; and H.C. Frey and S.R. Patil, Identification and Review of Sensitivity Analysis Methods, *Risk Analysis* 22(3) (2002): 553-578.

The QMU methodology, as just outlined, is applied to the weapons in the stockpile, and the M/U values of a range of critical performance gates are used as one input to judge the reliability of the warhead being assessed. For those components or characteristics that would have required a nuclear test for assessment, simulations are necessary. By using the simulation codes to predict changes in thresholds and uncertainties as components age, estimates can be made of how the performance of the warhead will change over time. Finally, the QMU framework is expected to play an important role in the certification of the reliable replacement warhead design. The objective is to quantify the margins and uncertainties of critical components and performance metrics in order to help determine whether the RRW designs can be certified to operate as intended.

Study Process

The study committee met first in May 2007 to discuss the charge and background with staff of the Government Accountability Office and NNSA. Briefings were also given by study committee members on the JASON QMU study. In addition, the committee formulated a set of issues to explore directly with the national security labs.

In August and September 2007, the study committee met with experts at the three national security labs—SNL, LANL, and LLNL. During those meetings, detailed presentations were provided on QMU methodology, examples of the application of QMU to weapons components and weapons systems, and, in the case of LLNL, the use of QMU to help with certification of the proposed RRW design. Presentations were made by management and by the staff members responsible for putting the QMU framework into practice on stockpile issues to provide views from both perspectives. A feature of these meetings was a series of roundtable discussions with designers about a broad range of QMU-related issues as seen by the practitioners.

In October 2007 and again in February 2008, the study committee spent most of its time in closed session arriving at findings and recommendations and writing the report. At both meetings, it also heard from the DOE Undersecretary for Science, Raymond Orbach, who presented some concerns about QMU as currently applied by the two design labs. Officials from the two design labs also attended the February meeting and spoke about their reactions to Dr. Orbach's concerns. A final meeting of a small group of the committee took place in April to complete a draft of the report. Because of the classified nature of the report, all report writing and subsequent report review had to be done in secure facilities. Upon completion of the report review, the document underwent a classification review by NNSA classification officials.

In addition, the study committee had access to a wide range of published documents about QMU, including all available reviews of its implementation by the laboratories.[17] Both unclassified and classified (at the secret restricted data level) material were made available to the committee.

---

[17]See, for example, D.H. Sharp and M.M. Wood-Schultz, QMU and Nuclear Weapons Certification: What's Under the Hood? *Los Alamos Science* 28 (2003): 47-53; and M. Pilch, T.G. Trucano, and J.C. Helton, *Ideas Underlying the Quantification of Margins and Uncertainties (QMU): A White Paper*, SAND2006-5001, Albuquerque, N.M.: Sandia National Laboratories (2006).

2

Use of the QMU Methodology

Task 1: Evaluate the use of the quantification of margins and uncertainties methodology by the national security laboratories, including underlying assumptions of weapons performance, the ability of modeling and simulation tools to predict nuclear explosive package characteristics, and the recently proposed modifications to that methodology to calculate margins and uncertainties.

> Finding 1-1. Quantification of Margins and Uncertainties (QMU) is a sound and valuable framework that aids the assessment and evaluation of the confidence in the nuclear weapons stockpile.[1]
>
> - QMU organizes many of the stockpile stewardship tools already in use, such as advanced simulation and computing (ASC) codes and computing, archival data, and aboveground experiments on both large and small facilities.
> - Aboveground experiments are critical in validating the ASC codes.
> - QMU does not replace existing assessment methodologies but extends their usage in a systematic manner.
> - QMU aids the national security laboratories in allocating important stockpile stewardship resources.

---

[1] The first number of the findings and recommendations numbering system refers to the task number with which the finding or recommendation is associated.

- **QMU could facilitate the communication of weapons system performance information to the Department of Defense (DOD) and Congress.**

QMU extends the concept of classic engineering factors that compute the ratio of design load to maximum expected load. Its use brings a systematic, quantitative approach to thinking about margins, M, and uncertainties, U. Using QMU, the national security laboratories can identify the factors and uncertainties that are most important to warhead performance. Resources can then be devoted to improving reliability and confidence based on those results.

From its investigations, the committee determined that QMU offers the following benefits:

- Its use has led to a greater emphasis on quantifying uncertainties in weapons performance to complement the national security labs' long-standing emphasis on quantifying margins.
- It allows performance margins to be managed as a system. This in turn allows designers to better evaluate the interconnections among components of the system and to answer quantitatively questions such as How much margin is enough? or How much uncertainty can be tolerated? QMU allows weapons designers and managers to consider trade-offs among schedule, cost, and performance. It is being used to guide investment decisions for both R&D and stockpile stewardship.
- It enables designers to monitor aging weapons and compare designs. The confidence ratio, M/U, is most effective for assessing the performance by tracking changes in it over time. For example, determining M/U as a function of the age of gas in the gas bottle can let the designers decide when the bottle must be replaced. It should be noted that the QMU methodology is likely to evolve over time as well, possibly faster than the changes that occur in aging warheads. To the extent such changes might affect the value of time-dependent measurements, these changes need to be accounted for when using QMU to monitor aging weapons.
- It is helping to improve communication among weapons designers, national security laboratory managers, and the three laboratories. It is also being used to explain the annual assessment process to nontechnical audiences, including senior DOE managers, senior DOD officials, Congress, and other external customers.
- An ongoing purpose of the science campaigns of the weapons program is to reduce uncertainties. QMU is applied in a snapshot mode when stockpile assessments are made in order to quantify

the uncertainties that exist at that time. Sensitivity studies allow one to guide and prioritize the application of effort to further reduce uncertainties.

It is important to remember, however, that QMU alone cannot enable the assessment or certification of a nuclear warhead. It complements and organizes but does not replace the assessment and certification methods developed in decades past. Some combination of surveillance, enhanced surveillance, statistical testing, enhanced aging experiments, testing to failure, significant findings investigations, and other methods directed and interpreted by experienced warhead design experts will always be a part of the QMU framework.

Recommendation 1-1a. The national security laboratories and NNSA should be encouraged to expand their use of QMU while continuing to develop and improve the methodology.[2]

Recommendation 1-1b. The laboratories and NNSA should strive to improve the connections between advanced simulation and computing programs and experimental programs.

Experiments are essential for quantification of uncertainties in simulation results. Coordination of experimental and computational programs can enhance the benefits of each. Coordination between the advanced simulation and the experimental programs at the laboratories has improved, but further improvement is possible and desirable.

UNCERTAINTY QUANTIFICATION

Finding 1-2. The national security laboratories have focused much of their effort for uncertainty quantification on computing the sensitivity of code output to uncertainties in input parameters. A broader effort is necessary. Methods for the identification, quantification, aggregation, and propagation of uncertainties require further development.

The laboratories have always been concerned with margins, M; QMU has appropriately placed emphasis on also quantifying uncertainties.

---

[2] Findings and recommendations are numbered to associate recommendations with their corresponding findings. For example, Recommendations 1-1a and 1-1b are associated with Finding 1-1, and Recommendation 1-2 is associated with Finding 1-2. Findings 1-3 and 1-6 have no associated recommendations.

There are serious and difficult problems to be resolved in uncertainty quantification, however, including physical phenomena that are modeled crudely or not at all, the possibility of unknown unknowns, lack of computing power to guarantee convergence of codes, and insufficient attention to validating experiments.

At the heart of uncertainty quantification efforts are today's modern simulation codes. Many factors, however, limit their ability to accurately simulate warhead performance. These factors, each of which introduces uncertainty to any code-calculated quantity, include the following:

1. Some physical phenomena remain unmodeled, including phenomena that have been recognized as potentially important. There may also be unmodeled phenomena that have not been recognized as important.
2. Some physical phenomena are modeled only crudely.
3. Even the most advanced supercomputers of today and the near future lack the memory and speed to permit numerically converged simulations using the best physics models in the codes.
4. The input data needed by the physics models are not known with perfect precision.
5. Only limited experimental data are available for assessing the accuracy of simulated quantities of interest.

UNCERTAINTY PROPAGATION AND AGGREGATION

The uncertainty introduced by each factor above is difficult to quantify or even to rigorously bound. Further, it is difficult to propagate and correctly aggregate the uncertainties arising from the myriad sources. The state of the art at the design labs is approximately as follows:

- Given sufficient computational resources, the labs can sample from input-parameter distributions to create output-quantity distributions that quantify code sensitivity to input variations. However,
  —Resources are not sufficient to do this with high fidelity;
  —Sampling from the actual high-dimensional input space is not a solved problem and is not done in the nuclear weapons context;
  —Often the unstated premise is that imperfect code is somehow good at calculating sensitivities to input variations.
- Discretization errors are not estimated in practice, and if they were, the machinery does not exist to propagate them and estimate the uncertainties that they generate in output quantities.

- Errors introduced by subgrid models are not estimated or propagated.
- Overall integrated physics-model errors are estimated by comparing post-shot simulation output against measured data, often from underground nuclear tests, with knobs set to values that the code users believe are reasonable and that best fit some chosen data set.
- Even if the uncertainties arising from all of the different sources were estimated, their aggregation into an overall uncertainty for a given quantity of interest is a problem that needs further attention.

Recommendation 1-2. The national security laboratories should continue to focus attention on quantifying uncertainties that arise from epistemic uncertainties such as poorly modeled phenomena, numerical errors, coding errors, systematic uncertainties in experiment.

Because discretization errors, code errors, and subgrid-model errors (poorly modeled physical phenomena) are not separately quantified, they are effectively lumped with errors in the physics models. As a result, differences between simulation and experiment may be attributed to one kind of error when in fact another kind is responsible. (More information on this topic is included in Note 1 in the classified Annex.)

The lesson is that unquantified numerical (and other) errors can lead to erroneous conclusions about important physics and to costly wasted effort. Unraveling the effects of numerical error (from insufficient resolution or from roundoff, for example) and model error (from poorly modeled real physical phenomena) continues to be an important unmet need.[3] One lesson learned from modern advanced simulation and computing codes is the critical importance of modeling turbulence, so important for mix phenomena, in three dimensions instead of one or two.

SOURCES OF UNCERTAINTY

Finding 1-3. In characterizing uncertainties it is important to pay attention to the distinction between those arising from incomplete

---

[3]See, for example, P.J. Roache, *Verification and Validation in Computational Science and Engineering*, Albuquerque, N.M., Hermosa Publishers (1998); T.G. Trucano, L.P. Swiler, T. Igusa, W.L. Oberkampf, and M. Pilch, Calibration, Validation, and Sensitivity Analysis: What's What, *Reliability Engineering and System Safety* 91(10-11)(2006): 1331-1357; and American Institute of Aeronautics and Astronautics, *AIAA Guide for the Verification and Validation of Computational Fluid Dynamics Simulations*, Reston, Va.: AIAA G-077-1998 (1998).

knowledge ("epistemic," or systematic) and those arising from device-to-device variation ("aleatory," or random).

Another issue that arises in assessing and communicating uncertainties in simulated quantities is that these uncertainties have at least three sources:

1. Uncertainty in our knowledge of properties of materials (including cross sections, opacities, etc.),
2. Differences between as-built and as-modeled devices (geometry, composition, initial conditions, etc.), and
3. Differences between the code (model plus numerical error plus bugs) and reality.[4]

If M is large relative to U for some performance metric, there may be no need to differentiate the portion of U arising from each source. If M and U are close, however, such differentiation may be important.

A simple (contrived) example illustrates the importance of keeping the first and second sources separate. Consider two hypothetical scenarios:

- *Scenario A.* The device design, combined with our excellent knowledge of nature's constants, is such that our uncertainty in those constants produces a very small uncertainty in device performance. Because manufacturing tolerances are loose, however, they or other factors can cause significant device-to-device variability. As a result, analysis and testing indicate that 90 percent of the device population will meet design requirements and 10 percent will fail to meet design requirements.
- *Scenario B.* The design and manufacturing tolerances are such that the device-to-device variability is very small. Basically, either all of the devices work or all fail. Uncertainties in the value of the properties of the device's materials, however, lead to significant variation in calculated performance relative to design requirements. As a result, analysis shows that 90 percent of the realistic input space (describing possible values of nature's constants) maps to acceptable performance, while 10 percent maps to failure. This 90 percent is a confidence number arising only from our lack of knowledge of nature's constants. Based on this limited knowl-

---

[4]See, for example, A. Mosleh, N. Tsiu, and C. Smidts, Model Uncertainty: Its Characterization and Quantification, *Proceedings of Workshop I in Advanced Topics in Risk and Reliability Analysis*, NUREG/CP-0138, Washington, D.C.: U.S. Nuclear Regulatory Commission (1994).

edge we have a 90 percent confidence that all devices will meet requirements and a 10 percent confidence that all will fail to meet requirements.

These two contrived scenarios lead to significantly different consequences. In Scenario A, the probability of at least one device succeeding can be increased to 99 percent by using two devices. In Scenario B, however, nothing can increase the confidence of a success above 90 percent. A 10 percent chance that all devices fail presents different concerns than the knowledge that 10 percent of the devices will fail.

The committee uses this (admittedly contrived) example to illustrate a potentially useful concept for communicating assessment results. This concept is taken from the probabilistic risk assessment community (see Appendix A) and is called the probability of frequency. In Scenario A we are highly confident that 90 percent of the devices will succeed. This translates to a nearly 100 percent probability that the frequency of success is 0.9. This is depicted graphically in Figure 2-1. In Scenario B, there is a 90 percent probability that the frequency of success is 1.0 and a 10 percent probability that it is 0.0.

In reality, the situation is not as sharply defined as in the committee's contrived example. Both types of uncertainty can exist simultaneously, and it is often difficult to separate them in the analysis. But as the examples illustrate, in some cases it may be very important to separate them to the extent possible, to recognize their different implications, and to devise a way to clearly communicate these important truths to the stakeholders.

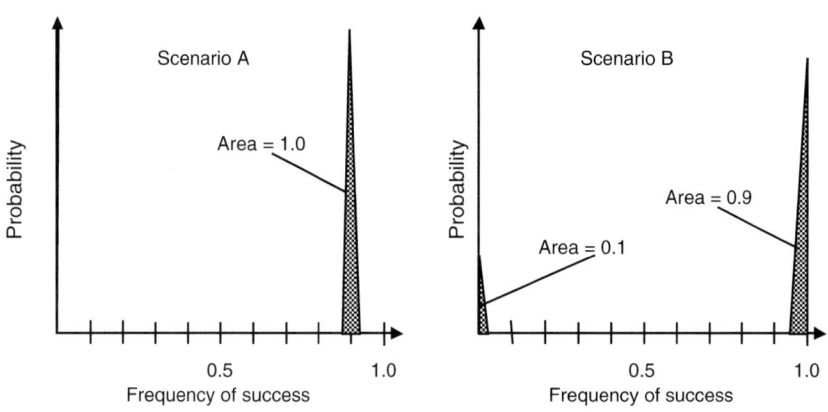

FIGURE 2-1 "Probability of frequency" for Scenarios A and B.

Consider, for example, the consequences for the stockpile if Scenario A pertains or Scenario B pertains.

The third source of uncertainty above is associated with model error. Assessment of the accuracy of a computational prediction depends on assessment of model error, which is the difference between the laws of nature and the mathematical equations that are used to model them. Comparison against experiment is the only way to quantify model error and is the only connection between a simulation and reality. If a particular experiment were perfectly characterized, measured data were free from error, and the mathematical model equations were solved perfectly, the difference between the mathematical solution and the experimental measurement would be the model error for the measured quantity. In practice the picture is muddied by imperfect characterization of experiments, imperfect measurements, numerical approximations of the mathematical model equations, and coding errors. Unless these factors are quantified and controlled, it is difficult to deduce model error, which in turn makes it difficult to assess the predictive capability of a simulation system.

Even if model error can be quantified for a given set of experimental measurements, it is difficult to draw justifiable broad conclusions from the comparison of a finite set of simulations and measurements. Importantly, if one has made comparisons for any set of experiments, it is not clear how to estimate the accuracy of a simulated quantity of interest for an experiment that has not yet been done. Said another way, it is not clear how to assess the proximity of a new problem to existing experimental experience or the likelihood that the simulation error for the next problem is similar to that for previous problems. Such assessments cannot be accomplished without heavy reliance upon expert judgment.

In the end there are inherent limits in the ability to quantify uncertainty. Such limits might arise from the paucity of underground nuclear data and the circularity of doing sensitivity studies using the same codes that are to be improved in ways guided by the sensitivity studies.

REPRESENTATION OF A SIMPLE PERFORMANCE GATE

Finding 1-4. There is much more to QMU than one or a few margin-to-uncertainty (M/U) ratios. By themselves, these ratios cannot convey all of the information needed for proper assessment, nor can one or a few probability distributions.

A performance gate is represented by a range of values for some performance metric that must be achieved for success. A performance threshold, on the other hand, is a value of a metric that must be exceeded to achieve success. The value of the threshold is uncertain, and the value

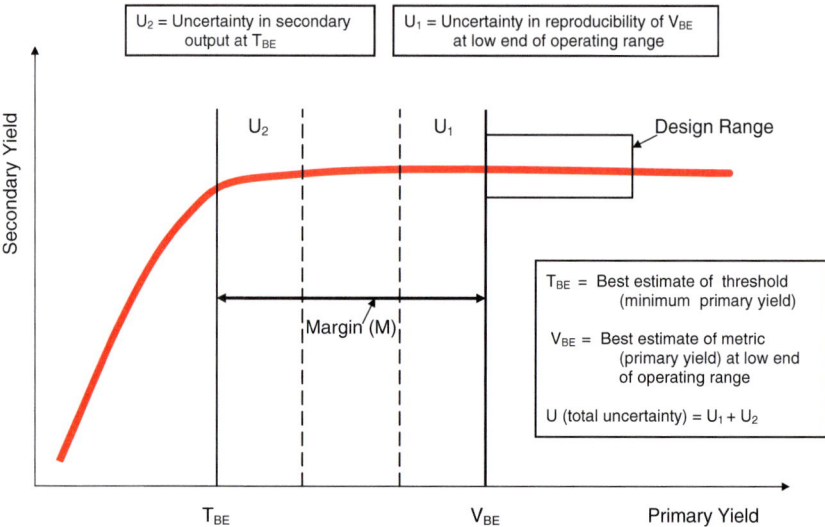

FIGURE 2-2 Cliff chart representation of warhead performance.

of the metric comes from calculations that are also uncertain. In this example (see Figure 2-2) the simplest use of QMU is to compare a single estimated number for a margin, M, against a single estimated number for the uncertainty, U.

Here M is the difference between the best-estimate value of the lower bound of the design range of metric V_{BE} (in the figure, the primary yield) and the best-estimate value of the upper bound of the threshold, T_{BE} (in the figure the minimum primary yield). U is the sum of two uncertainties. One, U_1, represents how much lower the metric's actual value, V_{true}, might be than its best estimate, and the other, U_2, represents how much higher the actual threshold, T_{true}, might be than its best estimate.

If one interprets $T_{BE} + U_2$ as the maximum credible value of the threshold and $V_{BE} - U_1$ as the minimum credible value of the metric, then one can interpret the difference $(V_{BE} - U_1) - (T_{BE} + U_2)$ as a measure of confidence or comfort that the performance gate has been passed. If the difference is positive—that is, if there is "white space" between the maximum credible threshold and the minimum credible metric value—there is some basis for confidence that the gate has been passed. The larger the difference is, the greater the confidence. We note that this difference is simply M − U and that a positive M − U means a ratio M/U that exceeds unity.

INTRODUCING MORE COMPLEX PROBABILITY DISTRIBUTIONS

The interpretations described above can be criticized on several grounds. First, taking $T_{BE} + U_2$ as the maximum credible threshold implies that the uncertainty in the threshold is bounded. This implication is equivalent to assuming that the distribution of threshold values arising from all sources of uncertainty does not have a significant tail. A similar comment applies to the metric value. Some observers argue that these distributions may have tails. Second, even if the distributions have finite extent, it may be difficult to demonstrate that U_1 and U_2 actually encompass the full extent of those distributions and thus that essentially 100 percent of the possible scenarios are within the given bounds. Third, even if U_1 and U_2 come from compact, finite distributions, the methods for estimating U_1 and U_2 contain assumptions, approximations, neglected factors, and other sources of uncertainty. It follows that the values of U_1 and U_2 are not precisely known. This calls into question the interpretations of "maximum credible value" and "minimum credible value."[5] In order for these uncertainties to be meaningful, they should be prescribed unambiguously. A commonly used measure is the number σ of standard deviations—such as 1σ, 2σ, or 3σ—of the uncertainty probability distribution. At the moment, there is no universally accepted definition at the laboratories of whether uncertainty refers to 1σ or 2σ (see Table 4-1).

How does one handle this? For a particular gate of interest, the laboratories interpret U_1 and U_2 as arising from distributions of finite extent and consider that the values they estimate are attempts to encompass the entire bound. However, they recognize the third criticism above and do not claim that $(M - U) > 0$ is sufficient but rather that $(M - U)$ should be significantly greater than zero (or M/U significantly greater than unity) in order to inspire confidence.

If the distributions have tails, and if one knows the type of distribution, it could be very helpful to quantify uncertainties in terms of standard deviations. This approach facilitates meaningful quantitative statements about the likelihood of successful functioning. For example, if the threshold distribution is normal and U_2 is its standard deviation ($U_2 = 1 \times \sigma_2$) and T_{BE} is assumed to be the mean, then we know that there is approximately a 16 percent chance that the true threshold, T_{true}, is greater than ($T_{BE} + U_2$). If the distribution of the metric values V is known, similar quantitative statements can be readily made about the likelihood

---

[5]To the extent (which is considerable) that input uncertainties are epistemic and that probability distribution functions (PDFs) cannot be applied to them, uncertainties in output/integral parameters cannot be described by PDFs. A bounding approach to the epistemic input uncertainties must be applied, and the output/integral uncertainties can only be bounded rather than being specified even in part by a PDF.

that $V_{true} < T_{true}$, which implies failure. This kind of statement is based on a knowledge of the actual shapes of meaningful distributions, of course, which may be difficult to find.

DIRECT COMPUTATION OF DISTRIBUTION OVERLAP

A similar approach that has been suggested is to compute distributions and use them directly—that is, without necessarily trying to identify values for M or U—to assess confidence that a performance gate is passed. This general idea appears to avoid some of the issues discussed above, such as how to rigorously define numbers such as M and U. The laboratories have computed distributions for several years as part of their sensitivity analyses, and they are evaluating how best to interpret them.

Particular attempts to implement this general idea[6] are also open to criticisms. First, they have not yet been shown, by analysis or demonstration, to be feasible with the full required scope and with present computing capability. Second, there is no obvious relation between confidence that a gate is passed and the specific metrics that have been proposed, such as the fraction of a given distribution that overlaps with some reference distribution or the width of a given distribution compared with a reference distribution. It could be challenging to devise a metric that does have the desired relation. Third, great care should be taken not to over- or misinterpret these distributions. Conclusions based on such misinterpretations could lead to harmful decisions. Fourth, there are questions about the meaning contained in the shape of these distributions, for they are direct results of the shapes of the distributions assumed for input parameters. In the presentations to the committee, the input distributions were simply uniform, meaning that each selected input value was considered just as likely as any other. The meaning of the shapes of the output distributions is not clear in this case. Fifth, there are similar questions about the meaning of the span of the distributions, which is a direct result of the span chosen for the input parameters as well as the particular (small set of) input parameters chosen for variation. If additional uncertain parameters are chosen, the width of the output distributions will almost certainly increase, the chosen metrics used to describe the distributions will change, and the conclusions drawn from the analysis also will likely change. If analysis results are sensitive to judgment-based choices of analysis inputs, then care should be taken to transparently show the effects of judgment on the results.

---

[6]Raymond Orbach, Undersecretary of Energy for Science, Presentations to the committee on October 26, 2007, and February 18, 2008.

Recommendation 1-4. The national security laboratories should further develop the QMU methodology to aggregate and propagate uncertainties. For full-system simulations, it is important to explore the validity and efficiency of alternative means of sampling the large input-parameter space to determine the expected performance output of the warhead and its uncertainty.[7]

Regardless of flaws in a particular distribution-based approach, the laboratories need to continue to evaluate a variety of approaches to quantifying confidence, including distribution-based approaches.[8] No single approach presented to date is without flaws; further work is needed to characterize and reduce these flaws.

Full system calculations are more commonly carried out using a staged computational approach[9] wherein it is necessary to be concerned with how uncertainties calculated in one stage (e.g., simulations of primary performance) using a sampling of input parameters are aggregated and/or propagated into the second-stage calculations (e.g., simulations of secondary performance). In the first stage, for example, uncertainties in pit mass and surface finish propagate to variations in cavity compactness; the latter then lead to variations in boost yield and, ultimately, variations in primary yield. Clearly, the imprint of a variation is carried through the entire first-stage calculation. These variations, however, do not propagate without designer intervention into a set of second-stage calculations (sec-

---

[7]See, for example, M.D. McKay, R.J. Beckman, and W.J. Conover, A Comparison of Three Methods for Selecting Values of Input Variables in the Analysis of Output from a Computer Code, *Technometrics* 21(2)(1979): 239-245; and J.C. Helton and F.J. Davis, Latin Hypercube Sampling and the Propagation of Uncertainty in Analyses of Complex Systems, *Reliability Engineering and System Safety* 81(1) (2003): 23-69.

[8]For example, evidence theory, possibility theory, and interval analysis. See, for example, T.J. Ross, *Fuzzy Logic with Engineering Applications*, 2nd ed., New York, N.Y.:Wiley (2004); T.J. Ross, J.M. Booker, and W.J. Parkinson (eds.), *Fuzzy Logic and Probability Applications: Bridging the Gap*, Philadelphia, Pa.: Society for Industrial and Applied Mathematics (2002); C. Baudrit and D. Dubois, Practical Representations of Incomplete Probabilistic Knowledge, *Computational Statistics & Data Analysis* 51(1)(2006): 86-108; and J.C. Helton, J.D. Johnson, and W.L. Oberkampf, An Exploration of Alternative Approaches to the Representation of Uncertainty in Model Predictions, *Reliability Engineering and System Safety* 85(1-3)(2004): 39-71.

[9]See, for example, R.J. Breeding, J.C. Helton, E.D. Gorham, and F.T. Harper, Summary Description of the Methods Used in the Probabilistic Risk Assessments for NUREG-1150, *Nuclear Engineering and Design* 135(1)(1992): 1-27; U.S. Nuclear Regulatory Commission, *Severe Accident Risks: An Assessment for Five U.S. Nuclear Power Plants*, NUREG-1150, Vols. 1-3, Washington, D.C.: U.S. Nuclear Regulatory Commission, Office of Nuclear Regulatory Research, Division of Systems Research (1990-1991); and J.C. Helton and R.J. Breeding, Calculation of Reactor Accident Safety Goals, *Reliability Engineering and System Safety* 39(2)(1992): 129-158.

ondary performance for a given primary input), which are carried out independently.

Ideally, a full-system calculation could have a range of input parameters (uncertainties) in the codes, in material equations-of-state, and in the specification of parts. A hands-off calculation for a particular choice from the enormous parameter set, for instance, gives as output a yield of the weapon. The uncertainties in output are then determined from a series of such full-system calculations, done by sampling the parametric spaces of input parameters. No compounding rule is needed for this approach.

Finding 1-5. QMU cannot be reduced to a black box of mathematical formulas. It relies upon expert judgment and will continue to do so for the foreseeable future.

The successful application of QMU requires a great deal of expert judgment from scientists and engineers with relevant weapons expertise—especially weapons designers—particularly in quantifying uncertainties.[10] This expertise is supported by advanced computer facilities. Several designers noted that expert judgment is based on experience; the number of experts with these capabilities will decline unless ongoing efforts to support necessary projects and experiments and to attract and retain quality staff continue to succeed.

Recommendation 1-5. To implement assessment methodologies such as QMU effectively, NNSA and the national security laboratories should explore all options to retain a quality staff of weapons designers, engineers, and computer scientists.

PHENOMENOLOGY OF NUCLEAR EXPLOSIONS

Finding 1-6. The identification of performance gates and the margin and uncertainty of each gate is incomplete. The application of QMU to some of the gates that have been identified is incomplete.

---

[10]See, for example, B.M. Ayyub, *Elicitation of Expert Opinions for Uncertainty and Risks*, Boca Raton, Fla.: CRC Press (2001); R.J. Budnitz, G. Apostolakis, D.M. Boore, L.S. Cluff, K.J. Coppersmith, C.A. Cornell, and P.A. Morris, Use of Technical Expert Panels: Applications to Probabilistic Seismic Hazard Analysis, *Risk Analysis* 18(4)(1998): 463-469; R.M. Cooke, *Experts in Uncertainty: Opinion and Subjective Probability in Science*, New York, N.Y.: Oxford University Press (1991); and S.C. Hora and R.L. Iman, Expert Opinion in Risk Analysis: The NUREG-1150 Methodology, *Nuclear Science and Engineering* 102(4)(1989): 323-331.

As a prelude to a discussion about performance gates, it is important to review some of the critical physics processes in a nuclear explosion and how they are simulated. These explosions produce the most extreme temperature, pressure, and radiation conditions encountered on earth. The multistep process that produces such an explosion cannot be observed directly. (More information on this topic is included in Figure B-I and Figure B-2 in the classified Annex.) Rather, knowledge of this process has been pieced together from physics understanding, experiments, full-scale nuclear tests (primarily underground nuclear tests), and expert judgment. (More information on this topic is included in Note 2 in the classified Annex.)

In the absence of a detailed physics understanding for these phenomena, the labs use four knobs (see Glossary) to represent them in the simulation models. (More information on this topic is included in Figure B-I in the classified Annex.) Each knob is a parameter in the simulation codes that can be adjusted to match important features of underground nuclear test data and of experiments on devices of similar design. Collectively, these four knobs represent the largest gap in scientific understanding of the nuclear explosive process. Much of the ongoing weapons physics work at the labs is focused on gaining a better understanding of the physics underlying these knobs. (More information on this topic is included in Note 3 in the classified Annex.)

ROLE OF MODELING AND SIMULATION IN QMU

In the QMU framework, modeling and simulation tools are used to determine the margins, M, for the various performance gates. They are also used in conjunction with experiments to estimate uncertainties, U. In addition, the effect that the performance at one gate has on the performance of downstream gates needs to be determined.

The performance gates must be considered by any of the methodologies that inform the QMU methodology. Performance gates can also be considered as checkpoints that assess the performance margins of key parameters as the explosion progresses. A similar list of safety and security gates and failure points is also required. (More information on this topic is included in Note 4 and Table B-1 in the classified Annex.)

Communications and transparency between the two labs would be enhanced if they were to draw up a comprehensive list of these gates and metrics. This point is discussed further in Chapter 4.

Finding 1-7. In the development and implementation of the QMU process, the national security laboratories are not taking full advan-

tage of their probabilistic risk assessment expertise. For example, the distinction made by probabilistic risk assessment experts between probability of frequency and probability is a concept believed to have merit in QMU applications. PRA concepts have demonstrated their value in assessing performance measures or gates such as safety and security and could contribute to making the assessment of weapons risk issues more transparent.

The committee observed that the national security laboratories have considerable expertise in probabilistic risk assessment, a discipline developed over the past several decades to facilitate the assessment of rare events for which there are limited data and testing results. The laboratories do not appear, however, to be drawing much on that expertise to supplement and possibly enhance the QMU process.[11]

Probabilistic risk assessment and QMU face similar challenges to quantify the risk and performance of complex systems for which testing results and data are very limited. In both cases, the quantification of uncertainties is essential but very difficult to do in a transparent manner (see Appendix A, prepared by study committee member B. John Garrick, for a more detailed discussion of how PRA might be able to contribute to the QMU process). While PRA has historically focused on the risk of system failures and current QMU efforts are primarily targeting nuclear weapons reliability, QMU must eventually address issues of safety and security. PRA concepts may help with this. Many concepts and ideas developed in the PRA field could contribute significantly to the QMU methodology in both reliability and risk applications, especially with respect to making the process more transparent. Examples are the "probability of frequency" concept for interpreting and presenting results (discussed in the example illustrated in Figure 2-1), the scenario approach for linking initiating events and initial conditions to events of interest, and methods of quantifying uncertainties.

Perhaps the biggest contribution that probabilistic risk assessment could make to enhance the QMU process would be a comprehensive PRA for each basic weapons system. The probability of frequency approach would be the best format for applying PRA because there is uncertainty

---

[11]See, for example, R.P. Rechard, Historical Relationship Between Performance Assessment for Radioactive Waste Disposal and Other Types of Risk Assessment, *Risk Analysis* 19(5)(1999): 763-807; U.S. Nuclear Regulatory Commission, *Reactor Safety Study—An Assessment of Accident Risks in U.S. Commercial Nuclear Power Plants*, WASH-1400 (NUREG-75/014), Washington, D.C. (1975); and W.H. Lewis, R.J. Budnitz, H.J.C. Kouts, W.B. Loewenstein, W.D. Rowe, F. von Hippel, and F. Zachariasen, *Risk Assessment Review Group Report to the U.S. Nuclear Regulatory Commission,* NUREG/CR-0400, Washington, D.C.: U.S. Nuclear Regulatory Commission (1978).

in the frequency with which any performance metric occurs. The resulting information and knowledge base could complement and contribute to the credibility of the QMU process. As noted in Appendix A, probabilistic risk assessments greatly expand the knowledge base of systems while facilitating their analysis and fundamental understanding.

> **Recommendation 1-7. The national security laboratories should investigate the utility of a probability of frequency approach in presenting uncertainties in the stockpile.**[12]

As noted in the simplified example illustrated in Figure 2-1 and further discussed in Appendix A, representing failure modes in terms of probability of frequency could provide decision makers with a richer understanding of the uncertainties—and a clearer notion of how to address them—than could estimating the reliability or M/U.

---

[12] See, for example, J.C. Helton and R.J. Breeding, Calculation of Reactor Accident Safety Goals, *Reliability Engineering and System Safety* 39(2)(1993): 129-158.

3

QMU and the Annual Assessment Review

Task 2: Evaluate the manner in which that methodology [QMU] is used to conduct the annual assessments of the nuclear weapons stockpile.

The annual assessment reviews serve as the means for the national security laboratories (LANL, LLNL, SNL) to communicate the assessed performance of the stockpile and whether to recommend a resumption of nuclear weapons testing. The reviews focus on specific weapons and are signed by the senior nuclear weapons officials at LANL and SNL or at LLNL and SNL, depending on which design lab is responsible for a particular weapon. Each annual assessment review describes the components covered by SNL and the appropriate design lab. The annual assessment reviews discuss results of closed significant findings investigations (SFIs), the significance of open SFIs, the evaluation of tests of specific components (e.g., of neutron generators), and the application of QMU analyses. Although QMU is an identified part of the annual assessment review process, it is not the only part and should not be viewed as the sole justification for the conclusions of the reviews.

> **Finding 2-1. The national security laboratories have increased the application of QMU to the annual assessment review. The inclusion of margins and uncertainties in the annual assessment review provides insight into the basis for confidence in stockpile performance, shows differences among the warhead types, and furnishes information specific to each weapons system. In the 2007 assessment,**

however, QMU is explicitly applied only to the (assumed) single-most-important performance measure for each stockpile warhead.

The 2007 annual assessment review was examined in depth by the committee. The use of QMU methodology in the annual assessment review is increasing, and that trend is expected to continue in 2008. The annual assessment reviews include discussions of issues involved in applying QMU and the different views of the national security laboratories where improvements are needed. In the 2007 annual assessment, uncertainty bands were developed using QMU formalism, whereas previously the labs had relied primarily on expert judgment. QMU has not yet been applied to safety, security, or human factors.

In the 2007 assessment, QMU was used to determine how the value and uncertainty of the anticipated primary yield, Y_p, compares with those of the minimum primary yield, $Y_{p,min}$, required for stable secondary performance.

The national security laboratories have made a good start in applying the QMU framework in the annual assessment reviews, but they acknowledge that they still have far to go. Margins, M, and uncertainties, U, should be reported for all critical performance gates.

The committee asked the labs to provide briefings on the use of QMU in the annual assessment process for three specific weapons systems: B61 (Sandia), W88 (Los Alamos), and W80 (Livermore). The use of QMU in these systems is summarized in the following sections.

SANDIA NATIONAL LABORATORIES

In the 2007 annual assessment review, SNL used QMU to assess the firing systems and neutron generators of the B61 system under normal, abnormal, and hostile (e.g., high radiation) environments as a function of component age. It also reported on the use of QMU to analyze the strong link/weak link system for the qualification of the W76 and the B83. For the 2008 annual assessment review, SNL will use a technical basis review team to help identify high-priority components for analysis.

SNL management reported that although its QMU assessments to date have been useful for obtaining a better understanding of margins, there is still a great deal of work to do to understand uncertainties. One senior manager noted that uncertainty quantification is a goal at this point, not a reality. SNL managers also reported that there is not much coordination among the national security laboratories on the selection of components for analysis except in one case: the degradation of neutron generators.

Nevertheless, management noted that the use of QMU has had two notable impacts. First, it is allowing the lab to move away from deterministic pass/fail criteria for component performance to more probabilistic criteria that address component performance as a function of age and other factors. Second, the shift to probabilistic approaches is also forcing the lab to reexamine the current bases for component performance requirements.

LOS ALAMOS NATIONAL LABORATORY

LANL briefed the committee on the application of QMU to assess margins and uncertainties in the primary and secondary of the W88. This system was designed for a high yield-to-weight ratio, which resulted in a small margin in the primary under the best of circumstances. The laboratory also reported that it has used QMU to assess primary margins and uncertainties in the W76 and an abbreviated QMU analysis to evaluate one-point safety of the B53.[1]

The laboratory noted that QMU has had specific benefits. LANL's application of QMU to the W88 primary resulted in two design changes that are expected to provide additional primary margin. Its use also allowed the laboratory to close a significant finding investigation (SFI) that had been open for 9 years. More generally, the use of QMU has motivated LANL to develop a common and transparent definition of minimum primary yield, $Y_{p,min}$, and has also enabled the lab to calculate what it calls "statistically defensible" uncertainty bands for $Y_{p,min}$.

LAWRENCE LIVERMORE NATIONAL LABORATORY

LLNL briefed the committee on the use of QMU for the W80 system. (More information on this topic is included in Note 5 in the classified Annex.) The laboratory has applied QMU to the primary and secondary of the W80, especially to assess temperature- and aging-related effects on primary and secondary performance. This work has been carried out in collaboration with LANL, which originally designed the nuclear explosive package.

LLNL reported that the use of QMU has had several benefits. On the W80, it resulted in a better understanding of margins and uncertainties in primary and secondary performance. It is also leading to the development of consistent approaches and definitions—for example, for $Y_{p,min}$ and uncertainty—at the lab and is helping to prioritize the lab's work on weapons systems.

Recommendation 2-1. The national security laboratories should continue to expand the application of QMU in annual assessments;

---

[1] The B53 is no longer in the stockpile.

in particular, M and U should be reported for more performance gates. In addition, the labs should investigate the benefits that cross-laboratory peer review of their use of QMU could provide for the annual assessment process.

PERFORMANCE GATES

The national security laboratories have made a good start in applying the QMU formalism, but they acknowledge that they still have far to go. An SNL representative, for instance, told the committee that it was "one percent QMU-ized" as of summer 2007. M and U should be reported for all performance gates that are judged to be critical. (More information on this topic is included in Table B-1 in the classified Annex.)

PEER REVIEW OPPORTUNITIES

The annual assessment process today begins at the responsible national security laboratories (LANL, LLNL, Sandia-Livermore, and Sandia-Albuquerque), with detailed analysis by the design and engineering team, followed by internal review at several levels, including review by a red team that brings in members from the other national security labs and from outside the labs. The responsible lab director is continuously involved in the process, and the final assessment requires the lab director's approval; it is then presented to the Secretary of Energy. Independently, the Strategic Advisory Group/Stockpile Assessment Team (SAG/SAT)[2] of the U.S. Strategic Command reviews the analysis by the design teams, together with DOD analysis, and presents its assessment to the Commander of the U.S. Strategic Command, who then reports to the Secretary of Defense. The two secretaries then transmit a letter to the President assessing the safety and reliability of the stockpile, along with a statement on the need for nuclear testing.

It has been suggested that these assessments be augmented by further assessments that are as independent of the weapons laboratories as possible and that are, to the extent possible, not lab-centric. The committee has considered this suggestion and offers the following observations. The expertise needed for the annual assessment of the nuclear explosive package resides primarily in the nuclear weapons science community. It

---

[2]The SAG/SAT tasking is to conduct annual assessments of the safety, security, and reliability of the nuclear weapons stockpile and to advise on the possible need for nuclear testing. The SAG/SAT membership includes retired nuclear weapons physics and engineering designers, weapons production managers, and flag officers formerly responsible for nuclear weapons operations.

is possible for an outside body to review the work approach used by the laboratories but not to perform its own analysis of lab-generated results. The committee notes that outside bodies (including SAG/SAT, which has retirees from the weapons-design community) do review the work. The committee is comfortable with outside bodies reviewing the approaches taken by the laboratories and advising them on alternatives; however, it believes that expert judgment remains an important ingredient of these assessments and that the required depth of expertise is found primarily in the nuclear weapons science community.

The committee strongly favors the idea of cross-laboratory peer reviews as part of the laboratories' assessments. Such peer review would augment current peer reviews internal to each laboratory and could bring a new level of independence, rigor, and confidence insofar as different codes, methodologies, and philosophies would be brought to bear on the assessment of a given warhead. This peer review should not dilute the three national security laboratories' accountability for the annual assessment reviews.

4

Comparison and Contrast of the Use of QMU

Task 3: Evaluate how the use of that [the QMU] methodology compares and contrasts between the national security laboratories.

Earlier reports[1] raised concerns that differences in the implementation of QMU among the three national security laboratories (both among the labs and among various groups within a single lab) could cause confusion and limit the efficacy of QMU as a framework for assessing and communicating the reliability of nuclear weapons.

> Finding 3-1. Differences in the implementation of QMU methodologies among the national security laboratories can be beneficial for promoting a healthy evolution of best practices. Sandia National Laboratories' requirements are different from those of the design labs, because many of their components can be extensively tested under many of the required conditions (unlike the design laboratories' nuclear explosive packages).[2]

---

[1] U.S. Government Accountability Office, NNSA Needs to Refine and More Effectively Manage Its New Approach for Assessing and Certifying Nuclear Weapons, GAO-06-261 (2006); U.S. Department of Defense, Report on the Friendly Reviews of QMU at the NNSA Laboratories, Defense Program Science Council, (March 2004).

[2] A slight revision in Finding 3-1 has been made to correct wording that mistakenly implied all of Sandia's components could be extensively tested. Other changes were made in the second paragraph of text following this finding.

Methods for implementing QMU continue to evolve, as they should, and the laboratories should explore different approaches as a means to determine the best approach for a given warhead. For example, LANL has focused on estimating uncertainties by a sensitivity analysis that examines the variations in simulated primary yield resulting from variations in input parameters (e.g., pit mass) for a given weapon. LLNL, on the other hand, has attempted to develop a comprehensive model that explains the test results for a variety of different primaries and thus addresses modeling uncertainties as well as parameter uncertainties.

Some differences in approach arise naturally from the different missions of the laboratories. For example, much of SNL's work is different from that of the design labs, because it involves warhead components other than the nuclear explosive package (e.g., the firing set and the neutron generator). In principle, SNL can test its systems under many of the relevant conditions; for these conditions SNL is not forced to rely on simulation codes to generate estimates of thresholds, margins, and uncertainties. For practical reasons, SNL cannot test statistically significant numbers of some of its components and therefore still uses computational modeling; however, the models can be challenged in many cases by full system tests. LANL and LLNL, on the other hand, cannot perform full system tests and must instead rely heavily on simulation codes in their assessments of margins and uncertainties. SNL also cannot test its components in "hostile" environments, in which the warhead is subjected to a nearby nuclear explosion, and thus much of its hostile-environment work shares many of the challenges faced by the design laboratories.

> **Recommendation 3-1. The national security laboratories should continue to explore different approaches—for example, using different codes—for QMU analysis for estimating uncertainties. These different methods should be evaluated in well-defined intra- and interlaboratory exercises.**

Differences in methodology are potentially positive, leading to healthy competition and the evolution of best practices. To determine a best practice, however, would require an ability to assess various competing practices. The committee has not seen an assessment of competing uncertainty quantification methodologies at any of the laboratories, nor has it even seen an organized attempt to compare them.

> **Finding 3-2. Differences in definitions among the national security labs of some QMU terms cause confusion and limit transparency.**

Table 4-1 shows that, in some cases, earlier concerns about inconsistencies continue to be valid. (More information on this topic is included

TABLE 4-1 Comparison of QMU Usage at the Nuclear Weapons Laboratories for the 2007 Annual Assessment

Item	Sandia Usage	Los Alamos Usage	Livermore Usage
Minimum primary yield, $Y_{p,min}$	N/A	• $Y_{tot} > 80\%$ • Valid model	• $Y_{tot} > 90\%$ • Valid model
Magnitude of U	One sigma	Two sigma	One sigma
Determination of U	Statistical observation	Various calculations and/or expert judgment	Various calculations and/or expert judgment
Figure of merit	K-factor[a]	M/U	M/U

[a] K = M/U with U measured at one sigma.

in Table B-2 in the classified Annex.) For example, in their presentations made to the committee, it became clear that researchers at LANL and LLNL were using different definitions of uncertainty (one sigma vs. two sigma) and different definitions of the important threshold $Y_{p,min}$ (minimum primary yield). The committee learned that the design labs have established a joint group on QMU and are working to establish common definitions and agreement on common metrics and failure modes, but clearly this is a work in progress. It is particularly important that common definitions be developed for parameters used in external communications.

Recommendation 3-2. To enhance transparency in communicating the results arising from the QMU analyses, national security laboratories should agree on a common set of definitions—such as the sigma level designating the magnitude of uncertainty—and terminology.

Inconsistencies in the definition of uncertainty and common terms such as $Y_{p,min}$ (minimum primary yield) are unnecessary and confusing and should be eliminated.

Finding 3-3. The consistency and transparency of the application of QMU are being inhibited by the lack of consistency within each lab and the lack of documentation.

In their presentations, NNSA and each of the laboratories told the committee that draft QMU guidance documents were being prepared by each organization. At this writing, however, none of these documents had been completed. The committee believes that documentation of the QMU approaches used by each lab (even in draft form), as well as overarching policy guidance on the implementation of QMU from NNSA, will be essential for improving consistency and transparency in the implementation of QMU and for facilitating peer review. Accordingly, documentation must be given high priority.

As noted above, the use of different approaches to QMU can be a strength as long as methods are documented to make them more transparent and to assist researchers in communicating effectively with one another, with management, and with outside audiences.

> **Recommendation 3-3. It is urgent that NNSA and the national security labs complete the development and issuance of QMU guidance documents in time for the current assessment cycle. This process should be used to drive consensus among lab scientists. The documents should be updated as the methodology matures.**

> **Finding 3-4. The QMU framework has yet to be clearly defined by the national security laboratories collectively or individually. This framework must identify a more comprehensive set of performance gates and describe how QMU is used to analyze each. A possible outcome of this process is that QMU is not appropriate for a particular performance gate.**

QMU is often conflated with the whole set of tasks and tools that must be carried forward for stockpile stewardship and design of the RRW. These tasks and tools exist independently of the way that QMU is defined. The tools used in the QMU process are, for the most part, already in widespread use; this is not the issue. Rather, the issue is that the overarching QMU process needs to take into account various divergent views on the essence of the process.

An incomplete QMU methodology could also result in a situation in which the blind application of QMU increases the likelihood of missing an alternative failure mechanism or of hiding it altogether. If this happened, efforts to increase a margin and improve the apparent confidence factor of a nuclear explosive package determined from the application of QMU could activate an alternative failure mechanism. For example, design changes that enhance yield margin could introduce one-point-safety concerns.

> **Recommendation 3-4. The national security labs should carry out interlaboratory comparisons of different methods for finding and characterizing the most important uncertainties and for propagating these uncertainties through computer simulations of weapons performance.**

5

QMU and the RRW Program

Task 4: Evaluate whether the application of the quantification of margins and uncertainties used for annual assessments and certification of the nuclear weapons stockpile can be applied to the planned Reliable Replacement Warhead program so as to carry out the objective of that program to reduce the likelihood of the resumption of underground testing of nuclear weapons.

From a historical perspective, there is evidence that some new nuclear warhead designs could be certified without nuclear testing. The Hiroshima bomb (Little Boy) was never tested before the military used it. The weapon tested at the Trinity site and used at Nagasaki (Fat Man) was of a quite different design. Designers could not accurately predict the yield to within limits acceptable at the present day, but they were within a factor of two of the actual yield, which is remarkable given that there were no test data on which to base their calculations.

Today's historical archive of approximately 1,200 U.S. nuclear tests provides an extensive database. Only a small fraction of the test archive is directly relevant to a particular warhead design, but the whole set has informed the design labs' understanding of the physics involved.[1] Further, that small fraction provides established reference points for performance (including tests with unexpected or even no nuclear yield).

---

[1] The entire archive provides the basis for what we have called "designer or expert judgment" in this report.

Given this knowledge and the archive of tests, a new nuclear weapon that is nearly identical to a tested existing design (such as the heavy B83 gravity bomb) and that needs only some relatively insignificant modification could be certified. All existing U.S. missile warheads, however, have smaller M/U ratios than the B83, because they were constrained to maximize yield while minimizing weight and size.

The first project in the RRW program was for a replacement missile warhead. The requirement for yield-to-weight ratio was relaxed considerably for the RRW competition, which enabled a design with substantially greater M/U ratio; this is the WR-1 design of LLNL.

Also relevant to the RRW program is legislation passed by Congress[2] that directed NNSA to begin a new Science Campaign called Advanced Certification, saying that "[Congress] believes the recent findings of the JASON group revealed significant systemic gaps in NNSA's stockpile certification process." The findings referred to are in a JASON report on the RRW.[3] In the legislation, NNSA is directed to report to Congress on Advanced Certification within six months of enactment; at this writing, the mandated report has not yet been issued. To give the reader an idea of what Advanced Certification might embrace, the study committee summarizes here Congress's direction for Advanced Certification:

1. Improvement of the weapons certification process through expanded, independent peer review mechanisms and refinement of computational tools and methods.
2. Advancement of the physical understanding of surety mechanisms.
3. Further exploration of failure modes.
4. Manufacturing process assessments.
5. The study of strategic system-level requirements.

Finally, Congress calls for NNSA to state in its report "progress [NNSA has] made in implementing the JASON's recommendations and improving the stockpile certification process." The JASON report specifically concerns RRW, but the committee believes that the intent of Congress is that Advanced Certification should apply to life-extension programs and annual assessments as well as to RRW. This observation is supported by recent Senate action on the FY2009 Energy and Water Development appropriations bill. In the report accompanying its bill, the Senate Appropriations Committee notes its continued support for the Advanced Certifi-

---

[2]U.S. Congress, Consolidated Appropriations Act, 2008, Division C—Energy and Water Development and Related Agencies Appropriations Act, 2008, House Appropriations Committee Print to accompany P.L. 110-161 (2008), p. 583.

[3]JASON, Reliable Replacement Warhead Executive Summary.

cation effort "to increase the safety and reliability margins of the stockpile without underground testing."[4]

Finding 4-1. QMU can be applied to the evaluation of any new designs, including the RRW, to contribute to enabling certification of those designs without nuclear tests.

QMU was used extensively in the design and certification plan for the WR-1. The approach taken in the WR-1 was to begin with tested designs and to then increase the primary yield to increase margin for driving the secondary while controlling uncertainties. (More information on this topic is included in Note 6 in the classified Annex.) Analyses to date have focused on two main performance issues: (1) primary boosting and (2) primary yield to drive the secondary.

The secondary design is based on solid principles of physics and engineering. Its ultimate certification will depend on further development, further analysis, and nonnuclear tests. (More information on this topic is included in Note 7 in the classified Annex.)

The current certification plan for WR-1 includes some key experiments to test and prove the design. These include three core-punch hydrotests and three pin dome shots. About 6 to 10 smaller hydrotests are for the fill tube and for parts of the radiation case. (More information on this topic is included in Note 8 in the classified Annex.) The committee observes that the schedule is success-oriented in that an unexpected failure in any of the major hydrotests could substantially delay the project. Confidence could be generated by designing an experiment that should lead to abnormal behavior and then actually seeing that behavior in the test. Which data are needed most can be determined using the QMU methodology to identify the physical models that engender the largest uncertainty. The experimental plan in support of WR-1 is of minimal extent, and because it assumes a high probability of success it does not adequately provide for resolution of test anomalies.

Finding 4-2. Any certifiable RRW weapons design will have to be "close" to the archival underground nuclear test base, while meeting reasonable criteria for adequate margin. The design and certification of new nuclear weapons that are sufficiently "close" to particular legacy designs could, in principle, be accomplished without nuclear tests, based on the existing nuclear test archive, on new experiments with no nuclear yield, and on modeling and

---

[4]U.S. Congress, Senate, 2008. S. Report 110-416, pp. 121, 146.

simulation tools supported by a QMU methodology more mature than at present.

For a certifiable RRW, the design labs will have to make the case that a new design is "close enough" to tested designs. The case would depend on establishing that the design is based on well-understood principles of nuclear warhead physics and engineering, that the design is related in key ways to designs that were successful in archived historical nuclear testing, and that any gaps between the knowledge of physics and engineering and the archival underground nuclear test base are bridged by experiments. Interpolation is highly preferable to extrapolation.

Recommendation 4-2. The design laboratories should lay out in detail their arguments for the relevance and closeness of archival underground tests to any proposed RRW design. These laboratories should investigate methodologies for helping address the problem of quantifying closeness.

How to transparently define and quantify "closely related" is a difficult issue to which the labs should devote sufficient effort. "Close enough" depends on the direction of the change as well as the magnitude—the direction should be away from "cliffs," and expert designer judgment must go into assessing "close enough." Prior warhead anomalies and their "fixes" should be used to validate the definition of "close enough." The goal is to increase the critical margins while controlling the uncertainties so that M/U ratios are greater than 3 or so. The margins and cliffs here are intentionally spoken of in the plural because there are multiple failure modes, and increasing one margin might decrease another—for example, increased Pu mass might endanger one-point safety, so all must be considered together. A primary lying between two successfully tested designs (i.e., interpolated rather than extrapolated) can provide additional confidence. The design and certification of new nuclear weapons that are sufficiently "close" to particular legacy designs could, in principle, be accomplished without nuclear tests, based on the existing nuclear test archive, on new experiments with no nuclear yield, and on modeling and simulation tools supported by a more mature QMU methodology.

It must be noted, however, that there is no commonly accepted quantification of closeness in the laboratories. While closeness will always have a substantial qualitative component based on expert judgment, a quantitative measure is clearly needed. This is not a trivial problem. While this committee is not in a position to offer a credible solution, it believes that any such solution will involve both QMU methodology and expert judgment. It also believes that it is possible to devise simulation tools that can help materially in quantifying closeness. There are presently many probabilistic approaches to closeness, such as Mahalanobis[5] or Bhattacharyya[6] distance, which could be modified and used by the laboratories in their search for such a definition.

Finding 4-3. The relevant performance gates might be different for different designs.

There could be new failure modes if new features are added. The M/U values of the old subsystems might change and new subsystems might then dominate the M/U. Further, the incorporation of surety features could create a situation in which new performance metrics would be needed to establish confidence that the design is not near a failure threshold.

Recommendation 4-3. The design labs should carefully examine all of the failure mechanisms for new RRW designs, criteria for the RRW to pass all performance gates, and the methodology used for these analyses.

As an example of problems that might arise in new designs, the addition of Pu mass to a primary design in order to increase the margin of the primary yield, Y_p, performance gate might decrease margin at the one-point safety gate. (More information on this topic is included in Note 9 in the classified Annex.)

Finding 4-4. A higher level of peer review, documentation, and experimentation without nuclear testing are essential to a credible RRW certification process.

For credible certification, the labs need to document the design and its analysis thoroughly and transparently, via QMU methodology, so that outside experts can independently judge its correctness and evaluate its credibility. The labs also need to track and document changes in design and reasoning by a version-control process. The evolution of the design is important evidence for the viability of the design.

Peer review is essential to credibility. Assessment and certification, with or without nuclear tests, are based on credibility. A strong peer review process, however, is not simply a step tacked on at the end of a design process. It is built into the process by taking steps throughout that

---

[5] Available at http://eom.springer.de/M/m062130.htm.
[6] Available at http://eom.springer.de/B/b110490.htm.

make the data and reasoning more transparent. QMU shares similar goals and, once implemented thoroughly, will much more readily support peer review. The laboratories have long practoied lab-vs.-lab review of designs. The committee suggests a stronger and more independent review process than that used for previous nuclear weapons, by engaging experts not directly involved in the project—that is, it remains lab vs. lab but now includes outsiders such as retirees and, perhaps, British experts—who can knowledgeably assess the design process and who can use their own simulation codes and analysis methods. For this peer review to affect the design, it must be timely.

Recommendation 4-4. The NNSA and the design laboratories should ensure that the certification plan for any RRW is supported by strong, timely peer review and by ongoing, transparent, QMU-based documentation and analysis in order to acheive a confidence level necessary for eventual certification.

Appendixes

Appendix A

A Probabilistic Risk Assessment Perspective of QMU

B. John Garrick, Committee Member

PURPOSE

It is the purpose of this appendix to consider if the several decades of experience with the application of probabilistic risk assessment (PRA) (Garrick, 2008), especially with respect to nuclear power plant applications, involve methods that might complement or benefit the QMU methodology. The quantification of margins and uncertainties (QMU) methodology refers to the methods and data used by the national security laboratories to predict nuclear weapons performance, including reliability, safety, and security. Both communities, PRA and QMU, have similar challenges. They are being asked to quantify performance measures of complex systems with very limited experience and testing information on the primary events of interest. The quantification of the uncertainties involved to establish margins of performance is the major challenge in both cases. Of course the systems of the two communities are very different and require system-specific modeling methods. To date the emphasis in the QMU effort has been on a reliability prediction process, not yet the important performance measures of safety and security. PRA focuses on what can go wrong with a system and thus could be an ideal method for assessing the safety and security of nuclear weapon systems.

NOTE: This Appendix was authored by an individual committee member. It is not part of the consensus report. The appendix provides a description of PRA and probability of frequency concepts that are discussed in the report.

The approach taken in this review is to highlight the PRA method of quantification, comment on applying PRA to weapon performance assessment, discuss possible links and differences between QMU as currently used and PRA, and to identify possible PRA enhancements of QMU. The QMU approach itself is covered elsewhere in this report.

THE PRA APPROACH TO QUANTIFICATION

The PRA approach highlighted is based on the framework of the triplet definition of risk (Kaplan and Garrick, 1981):

$$R = \{<S_i, L_i, X_i>\}_c,$$

where R denotes the risk attendant on the system or activity of interest. On the right, S_i denotes the ith risk scenario (a description of something that can go wrong). L_i denotes the likelihood of that scenario happening and X_i denotes the consequences of that scenario if it does happen. The angle brackets < > enclose the risk triplets, the curly brackets { } are mathspeak for "the set of," and the subscript c denotes "complete," meaning that all of the scenarios, or at least all of the important ones, must be included in the set. The body of methods used to identify the scenarios (S_i) constitutes the "Theory of Scenario Structuring." Quantifying the L_i and the X_i is based on the available evidence using Bayes' theorem, illustrated later.

In accordance with this set of triplets definition of risk, the actual quantification of risk consists of answering the following three questions:

1. What can go wrong? (S_i)
2. How likely is that to happen? (L_i)
3. What are the consequences if it does happen? (X_i)

The first question is answered by describing a structured, organized, and complete set of possible risk scenarios. As above, we denote these scenarios by S_i. The second question requires us to calculate the "likelihoods," L_i, of each of the scenarios, S_i. Each such likelihood, L_i, is expressed as a "frequency," a "probability," or a "probability of frequency" curve (more about this later).

The third question is answered by describing the "damage states" or "end states" (denoted X_i) resulting from these risk scenarios. These damage states are also, in general, uncertain. Therefore these uncertainties must also be quantified, as part of the quantitative risk assessment process. Indeed, it is part of the quantitative risk assessment philosophy to quantify all the uncertainties in all the parameters in the risk assessment.

Some authors have added other questions to the above definition such as What are the uncertainties? and What corrective actions should be taken? The uncertainty question is embedded in the interpretation of "likelihood," as noted later. The question about corrective actions is interpreted as a matter of decision analysis and risk management, not risk assessment per se. Therefore it is not considered a fundamental property of this definition of risk. Risk assessment does become involved to determine the impact of the corrective actions on the "new risk" of the affected systems.

Using the triplet definition of risk as the overarching framework, the following steps generally represent the PRA process:

> *Step 1.* Define the system being analyzed in terms of what constitutes normal or successful operation to serve as a baseline for departures from normal operation.
> *Step 2.* Identify and characterize what constitutes an undesirable outcome of the system. Examples are failure to perform as designed, damage to the system, and a catastrophic accident.
> *Step 3.* Develop "What can go wrong?" scenarios to establish levels of damage and consequences while identifying points of vulnerability.
> *Step 4.* Quantify the likelihoods of the different scenarios and their attendant levels of damage based on the totality of relevant evidence available.
> *Step 5.* Assemble the scenarios according to damage levels and cast the results into the appropriate risk curves and risk priorities.
> *Step 6.* Interpret the results to guide the risk-management process.

These six steps tend to collapse into the three general analytical processes illustrated in Figure A-1—a system analysis, a threat assessment, and a vulnerability assessment. That is, a PRA basically involves three main processes: (1) a system analysis that defines the system in terms of how it operates and what constitutes success, (2) an initiating event and initial condition assessment that quantifies the threats to the system, and (3) a vulnerability assessment that quantifies the resulting risk scenarios and different consequences or damage states of the system, given the possible threats to the system. A valuable attribute of the triplet approach is that it can track multiple end states in a common framework.

In Figure A-1 the system analysis is denoted as the "system states for successful operation." The second part of the process requires a determination of the threats to any part of the total system—that is, events

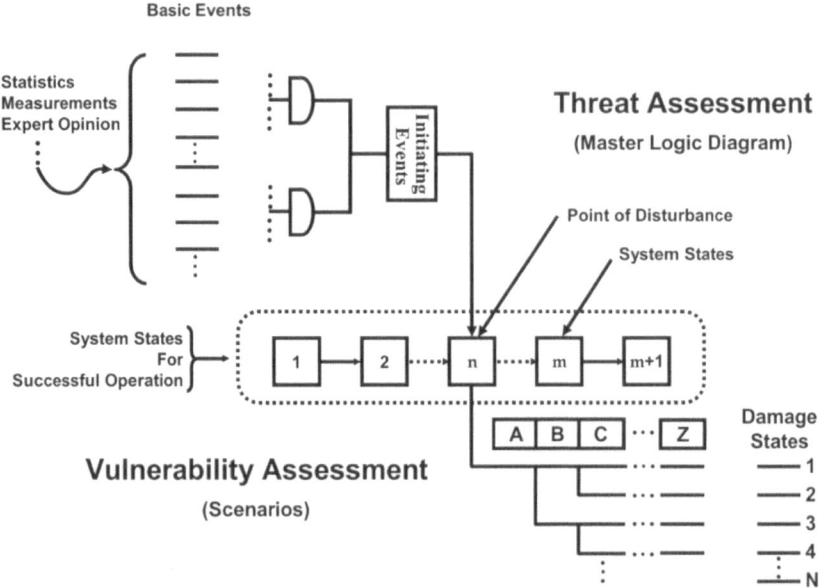

FIGURE A-1 The concept of an integrated threat and vulnerability risk assessment.

that could trigger or initiate a disturbance to an otherwise successfully operating system. The third part of the process structures the course and consequence of events (scenarios) that could emanate from specific initiating events or initial conditions.

A number of thought processes and analytical concepts are employed to carry out the three processes conceptualized in Figure A-1. They involve an interpretation of "likelihood," a definition of "probability," the algorithms of deductive and inductive reasoning, the processing of the evidence, the quantification and propagation of uncertainties, and the assembly of the results into an interpretable form. Some of the more important concepts are highlighted.

Three explicit and quantitative interpretations of likelihood are "frequency," "probability," and "probability of frequency."

- *Frequency.* If the scenario is recurrent—that is, if it happens repeatedly—then the question How frequently? can be asked and the answer can be expressed in occurrences per day, per year, per trial, per demand, etc.
- *Probability (credibility).* If the scenario is not recurrent—if it happens either once or not at all—then its likelihood can be quantified in terms of probability. "Probability" is taken to be synonymous

with "credibility." Credibility is a scale invented to quantitatively measure the degree of believability of a hypothesis, in the same way that scales were invented to measure distance, weight, temperature, etc. Thus, in this usage, probability is the degree of credibility of the hypothesis in question based on the totality of relevant evidence available.
- *Probability of frequency.* If the scenario is recurrent (like a hurricane, for example) and therefore has a frequency whose numerical value is not, however, fully known, and if there is some evidence relevant to that numerical value, then Bayes' theorem (as the fundamental principle governing the process of making inference from evidence) can be used to develop a probability curve over a frequency axis. This "probability of frequency" interpretation of likelihood is often the most informative, and thus is the preferred way of capturing/quantifying the state of knowledge about the likelihood of a specific scenario.

Having proposed a definition of probability, it is of interest to note that it emerges also from what some call the "subjectivist" view of probability, best expressed by the physicist E.T. Jaynes (2003):

> A probability assignment is 'subjective' in the sense that it describes a state of knowledge rather than any property of the 'real' world, but is 'objective' in the sense that it is independent of the personality of the user. Two rational beings faced with the same total background of knowledge must assign the same probabilities.

The central idea of Jaynes is to bypass opinions and seek out the underlying evidence for the opinions, which thereby become more objective and less subjective.

Recalling the interpretation of probability as credibility, in this situation, probability is a positive number ranging from zero to one and obeys Bayes' theorem. Thus, if we write $p(H|E)$ to denote the credibility of hypothesis H, given evidence E, then

$$p(H|E) = p(H) \frac{p(E|H)}{p(E)},$$

which is Bayes' theorem. It tells us how the credibility of hypothesis H changes when new evidence, E, occurs. Bayes' theorem is a simple two-step derivation from the product rules of probability and plausible reasoning. This theorem has a long and bitterly controversial history but in recent years has become widely understood and accepted.

A central feature of probabilistic risk assessment is making uncertainty an inherent part of the analysis. Uncertainty exists, to varying degrees, in all the parameters that are used to describe or measure risk. Of course there are sources of uncertainty other than parameter uncertainty, such as uncertainty about whether a particular phenomenon is being correctly modeled. A common approach to assessing modeling uncertainty is to apply different models to the same calculation in an attempt to expose modeling variability. Adjustments are made to the model to increase confidence in the results. The lack of confidence resulting from such an analysis can be a basis for assigning a modeling uncertainty component to parameter uncertainty in order to better characterize the total uncertainty of the analysis.

In PRA, parameter uncertainties are quantified by plotting probability curves against the possible values of these parameters. These probability curves are obtained using Bayes' theorem.

Before the risk scenarios themselves can be quantified, the initiating events (IE) or the initial conditions (IC) of the risk scenarios must be identified and quantified.[1] The relationship between the initial states (IEs and ICs), the system being impacted, and the vulnerability of the system being impacted is illustrated in Figure A-1.

A deductive logic model—that is, a fault tree or master logic diagram—is developed for each initiating event of a screened set. The structure of the logic model is to deduce from the "top events"—that is, the selected set of hypothetical IEs or ICs—the intervening events down to the point of "basic events." A "basic event" can be thought of as the initial input point for a deductive logic model of the failure paths of a system. For the case of accident risk, a basic event might be fundamental information on the behavior of structures, components, and equipment. For the case of a natural system such as a nuclear waste disposal site, a basic event could be a change in the ICs having to do with climate brought about by greenhouse gases. For the case of terrorism risk, the basic event relates to the intentions of the terrorist—that is, the decision to launch an attack. For the case of a nuclear weapon system, either environments or conditions could impact weapon performance. The intervening events of the master logic diagram for terrorism risk are representations of the planning, training, logistics, resources, activities, and capabilities of the terrorists. The intervening events of the master logic diagram for accident risk are the processes and activities that lead to the failure of structures, components, and equipment. The intervening events of the ICs for a nuclear waste disposal site could be factors that influence climate, and the intervening

---

[1]Both IE and IC terminology are used, since for some systems such as the risk of a nuclear waste repository the issue is not so much an initiating event as it is a set of initial conditions such as annual rainfall.

APPENDIX A

events for a nuclear weapon system could be environments that impact weapon yield.

Once the initiating events are quantified, the resulting scenarios could be structured to the undesired consequences or end states. The actual quantification of the risk scenarios is done with the aid of event trees similar to the one in Figure A-2. An event tree is a diagram that traces the response of a system to an initiating event, such as a terrorist attack, to different possible end points or outcomes (consequences). A single path through the event tree is called a "scenario" or an "event sequence." The terms are sometimes used interchangeably. The event tree displays the systems, equipment, human actions, procedures, processes, and so on that can affect the consequences of an initiating event depending on the success or failure of intervening actions. In Figure A-2 boxes with the letters A, B, C, and D represent these intervening actions. The general convention is that if a defensive action is successful, the scenario is mitigated. If the action is unsuccessful, then the effect of the initiating event continues as a downward line from the branch point as shown in Figure A-2. For accident risk, an example of a mitigating system might be a source of emergency power. For terrorism risk, an action that could mitigate the hijacking of a commercial airliner to use it as a weapon to crash into a football stadium would be a remote takeover of the airplane by ground control. For a natural system, a mitigating feature might be an engineered barrier, and for a nuclear weapon a mitigating system might be the shielding of external radiation.

Each branch point in the event tree has a probability associated with it. It should be noted that the diagram shown in Figure A-2 shows only two branches (e.g., success or failure) from each top event. However, a top event can have multiple branches to account for different degrees of degradation of a system. These branch points have associated "split

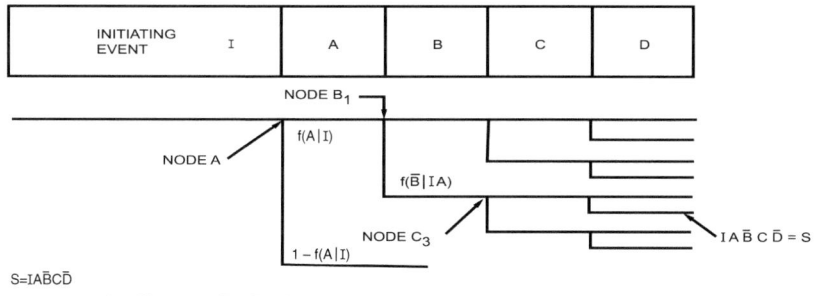

FIGURE A-2 Quantification of a scenario using an event tree.

fractions" that must be quantified based on the available evidence. The process involves writing an equation for each scenario (event sequence) of interest. For example, the path through the event tree that has been highlighted in Figure A-2 could be a scenario that we wish to quantify. The first step is to write a Boolean equation for the highlighted path. If we denote the scenario by the letter S, we have the following equation,

$$S = IA\bar{B}C\bar{D},$$

where the bars over the letters indicate that the event in the box did not perform its intended function. The next step is to convert the Boolean equation into a numerical calculation of the frequency of the scenario. Letting φ stand for frequency and adopting the split fraction notation, $f(\ldots)$, of Figure A-2 gives the following equation for calculating the frequency of the highlighted scenario:

$$\varphi(S) = \varphi(I)f(A|I)f(\bar{B}|IA)f(C|IA\bar{B})f(\bar{D}|IA\bar{B}C)$$

The remaining step is to communicate the uncertainties in the frequencies with the appropriate probability distributions. This is done using Bayes' theorem to process the elemental parameters (Figure A-3). The "probability of frequency" of the individual scenarios is obtained by convoluting the elemental parameters in accordance with the above equation.

Once the scenarios have been quantified, the results take the form shown in Figure A-4. Each scenario has a probability-of-frequency curve in the form of a probability density function quantifying its likelihood of occurrence. The total area under the curve represents a probability

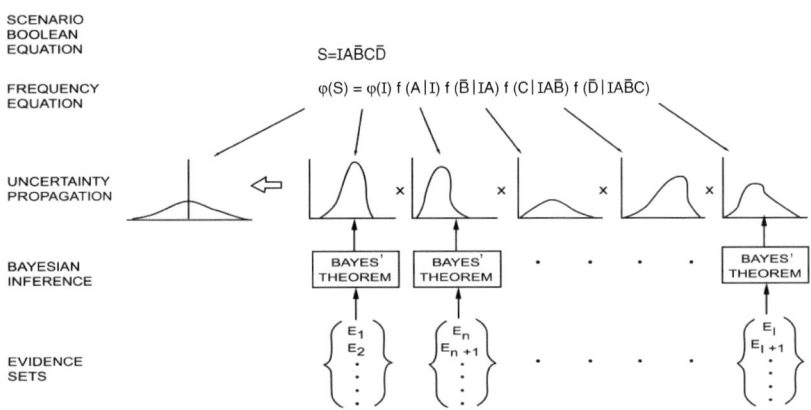

FIGURE A-3 Bayes' theorem used to process parameters.

APPENDIX A

of 1. The fractional area between two values of φ represents the confidence—that is, the probability—that φ has the values over that interval (see below).

Figure A-4 shows the curve for a single scenario or a set of scenarios leading to a single consequence. Showing different levels of damage, such as the risk of varying numbers of injuries or fatalities, requires a different type of presentation. The most common form is the classical risk curve, also known as the frequency-of-exceedance curve or the even more esoteric label, the complementary cumulative distribution function. This curve is constructed by ordering the scenarios by increasing levels of damage and cumulating the probabilities from the bottom up in the ordered set against the different damage levels. Plotting the results on log-log paper generates curves such as those shown in Figure A-5.

Suppose P_3 in Figure A-5 has the value of 0.95—that is, a probability of 0.95. We can be 95 percent confident that the frequency of an X_1 consequence or greater is φ_1. The family of curves (usually called percentiles) can include as many curves as necessary. The ones most often selected in practice are the 5th, 50th, and 95th percentiles. A popular fourth choice is the mean.

A common method of communicating uncertainty in the risk of an event is to present the risk in terms of a confidence interval. To illustrate confidence intervals some notation is added to the above figures, which now become Figures A-6 and A-7. If the area between φ_1 and φ_2 of Figure A-6 takes up 90 percent of the area under the curve, we are 90 percent confident (the 90 percent confidence interval) that the frequency is between φ_1 and φ_2. Figure A-7 can also be read in terms of a confidence interval. Let P_1 be 0.05, P_3 be 0.95, φ_1 be one in 1,000, φ_2 one in 10,000, and X_1 be 10,000 fatalities. Because P_3 minus P_1 is 0.90, we are 90 percent confident that the frequency of an event having 10,000 fatalities or more varies from one every 1,000 years to one every 10,000 years.

Although risk measures such as those illustrated in Figures A-6 and A-7 answer two questions—What is the risk? How much confidence is there in the results?—they are not necessarily the most important output

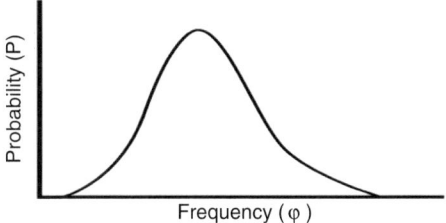

FIGURE A-4 Probability of frequency curve.

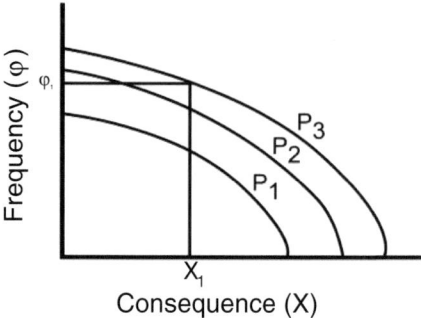

FIGURE A-5 Risk curves for varying consequences.

of the risk assessment. Often the most important output is the exposure of the detailed causes of the risks, a critical result needed for effective risk management. The contributors to this risk are buried in the results assembled to generate the curves in Figures A-6 and A-7. Most risk assessment software packages contain algorithms for ranking the importance of contributors to the risk.

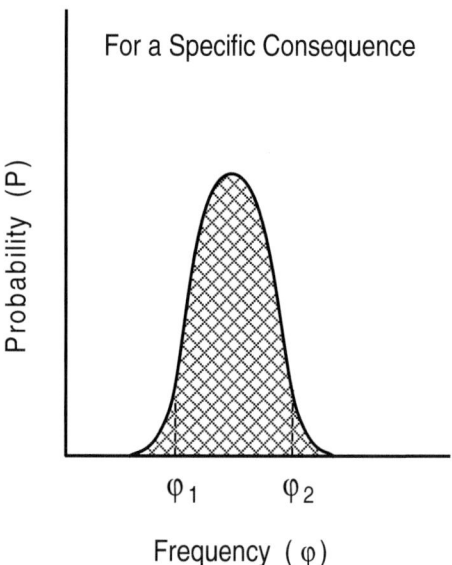

FIGURE A-6 Probability density.

APPENDIX A 61

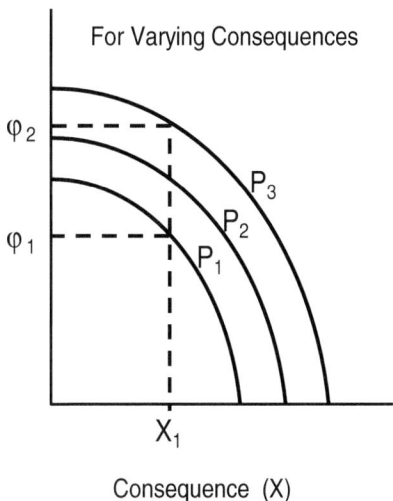

FIGURE A-7 Cumulative probability.

APPLYING PRA TO WEAPON PERFORMANCE ASSESSMENT

Since the probabilistic risk assessment was developed to apply to any type of risk assessment, it is believed that it could be a framework for assessing the risk in any type of system, natural or engineered, weapon or nonweapon. However, it could not be applied to nuclear weapons without using the whole host of computer codes and analytical processes that have been developed to support the current efforts for the quantification of margins and uncertainties methodology developed by the national security laboratories. In fact, because of the advanced state of development of the laboratory codes for calculating confidence ratios of performance margins and uncertainties, the most prudent use of the PRA thought process is probably for safety and security issues and elements such as the impact on weapon performance of stockpile storage or other events associated with the stockpile-to-target sequence. In fact, these elements could be the major contributors to the risk of poor weapon performance.

In general, PRA methods have been successfully applied to nonwarhead operational elements of the nuclear weapon functional life cycle. This still leaves open the question of how PRA might be used to quantify the risk of less-than-acceptable performance of a nuclear warhead. Providing a full answer to this question is beyond the scope of this appendix, but it is possible to describe the concept.

Suppose as a part of an assessment of the risk of a warhead not

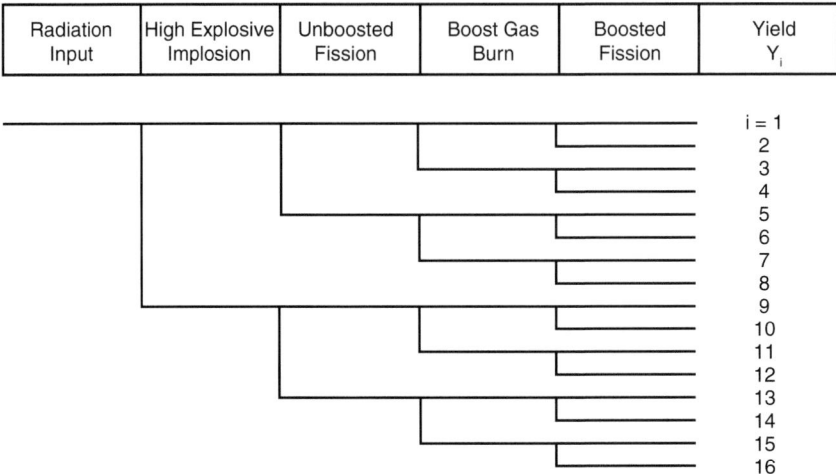

FIGURE A-8 Single-stage boosted fission explosive event tree.

performing to its specification, consideration is given to the risk of the weapon's primary explosion performance being compromised by external radiation. (More information on this topic is included in Note 11 in the classified Annex.) In particular, an initiating event is defined as the frequency per mission hour of an external radiation pulse of sufficient energy to impact weapon performance. The frequency of such an event would have to be based on multiple sources of evidence, including the state of the technology for defensive systems (which could, for example, come from intelligence reports), the mitigation capability of the weapon system itself, evasive procedures, mission conditions, etc. To be sure there would be uncertainties, which means that the frequency would have to be represented by a probability distribution in "probability of frequency" format. Figure A-8 is a conceptual interpretation of the events that would have to successfully occur for a single-stage boosted fission explosive to perform its intended function.

The event tree identifies the possible pathways triggered by the initiating event. The end states are a range of primary yields of the different event sequences (scenarios). Of course, the physics of the process will lead to many of the branch points being bypassed and the number of outcome states being reduced. The events may be briefly described as follows:

- *Radiation input.* An external radiation source impinged on the weapon system. The event is represented as a frequency per mis-

sion hour of an external radiation pulse of sufficient energy to impact weapon performance.
- *High explosive implosion.* If the radiation fluence impinging on a boosted fission explosive is varied, the performance of the device will vary.
- *Unboosted fission.* The degraded performance of the high explosive implosion will reduce the criticality of the explosive fissionable material and reduce the amount of fission energy generated before the boost stage.
- *Boost gas burn.* The boost is dependent on a sufficient amount of fission energy to heat and compress the boost gas to thermonuclear fusion conditions. The number of boost neutrons produced is affected.
- *Boosted fission.* The final yield is determined by the number of boosted fission events. Boosted fission scales with the number of boost neutrons available.
- *Yield.* The end states are probability of frequency (POF) distributions of different yields, including the design yield.

Having a POF distribution for each of these scenarios sets the stage for developing risk curves for a particular initiating event. The outputs of the event tree are calculated as described in the section "The PRA Approach to Quantification." The results from the event tree can be assembled into several different forms. One form would be to probabilistically add all the less-than-design-yield POF distributions to achieve the probability density curve for the risk of the primary not reaching its intended yield. This result would be in the form shown in Figure A-4, which characterizes the risk, including uncertainty, of this stage not performing to its specification.

A second form, if there are multiple degraded end states to be considered, would be to arrange the end state POF curves of the degraded yields in order of increasing degradation and cumulate them from the bottom to the top in the form of a complementary cumulative distribution function. The result is given in Figure A-5, which quantifies the risk of different degraded yields of single-stage boosted fission explosion with probability, P, as the parameter of the model.

A third form of presenting the results would be the POF curve representing the success scenario.

These three results represent a comprehensive set of metrics for measuring the performance with uncertainty of the primary fission explosion under the specific threat of a single initiator. To complete the risk assessment of the single-stage boosted fission explosive requires the consideration of all the important risk contributing initiators. Usually that is done by creatively defining a relatively small number of initiating event "categories" that represent several individual initiating events.

POSSIBLE LINKS BETWEEN QMU AND PRA

Among the common challenges to both the QMU and PRA methodologies is a convincing treatment of parameter and modeling uncertainty. Linking supporting evidence to the PRA and QMU calculations is critical to providing transparency and confidence in uncertainty analyses. Experience indicates that the key to uncertainty analysis is not so much data limitations as it is to have a system in place to capture and process the data and information that are often available but perhaps not easy to retrieve or in the proper form. Experience with nuclear power plant PRAs has shown this many times. For example, the systematic processing of maintenance and operations data has provided a robust database for assessing nuclear plant risk, which was thought to not be possible when PRAs were first implemented. Of course, this is not a database of many of the events of interest such as core melts or large releases of radioactive materials. Fortunately, not many such events have occurred. But, it is an important database for precursor events to these more serious events. If the precursor events where there are data are logically connected to the events of interest by detailed logic models, then the opportunity exists to appropriately propagate the uncertainties to the desired end states.

The nuclear weapons field would seem to be in a situation similar to that of the nuclear power field. While there is no actual testing being performed on full-scale nuclear weapons, data are being developed through precursor tests and weapons management activities. Nuclear explosive safety teams have been analyzing and observing assembly, disassembly, and repair activities for decades. An examination of this robust experience in nuclear weapons operations would seem to be similar to the experience in nuclear power maintenance and operations, especially with respect to safety and security issues. To be sure, many nuclear explosive safety activities go beyond the nuclear explosive package of nuclear warheads and some data needs of the nuclear explosive package are unique, thus limiting data collection opportunities. Nevertheless, it would appear that opportunities exist for large-scale data collection and processing in the weapons field. It is interesting to observe that both communities have benefited considerably by increased use of Bayesian methods to infer the performance characteristics of their respective systems' components.

APPENDIX A

APPARENT DIFFERENCES BETWEEN THE APPROACHES

One of the main differences between the two approaches (PRA and QMU), at least from an outsider's perspective, is the transparency of the performance assessment. The QMU assessments are packaged in a series of highly sophisticated computer codes that have a history of many decades. These codes represent the legacy memory and expert systems of decades of experience in predicting weapon performance. The sophistication of the codes and the matter of security compromises their transparency. However, nuclear power is highly regulated, and the transparency of its safety analysis has always been an inherent requirement of the process. Thus, it is expected that the safety analysis methods for nuclear power plants would make the basic structure and results of the modeling highly visible and accessible.

Another difference between the two approaches is that, at present at least, they are trying to answer different questions. The QMU question is currently driven by a reliability perspective and PRA by a risk perspective. Of course, to understand reliability one must know what the risks are and vice versa. But they are different because the emphasis in the models is different. The final form of the results in the QMU approach is a reliability number and the final result in a PRA is the risk of damage and adverse consequences. Both approaches attempt to quantify margins of performance and the uncertainties involved. There will indeed be convergence to common goals as QMU begins to address more explicitly such issues as safety, security, the stockpile-to-target sequence, and stockpile aging.

POSSIBLE PRA ENHANCEMENTS OF QMU

This appendix started out with the goal of identifying possible enhancements of the QMU methodology as a result of the very large experience base in probabilistic risk assessment, especially in the case of nuclear power. Perhaps the biggest contribution that PRA could make to the QMU methodology would be a comprehensive PRA of each basic weapon system. Experience with PRA strongly supports the view that the information and knowledge base created in the course of performing the PRA could contribute to the credibility of the QMU process. Almost every phase of nuclear power plant operation has been favorably affected by PRAs, from maintenance to operating procedures, from outage planning to plant capacity factors, from sound operating practices to recovery and emergency response, and from plant simulation to operator training. It is logical to expect the same would be true for the QMU process, for conducting weapon performance assessments, and for carrying out the nuclear explosives safety process.

Some of the characteristics of PRA that might enhance the QMU process are (1) explicitness of event sequences (scenarios) leading to degraded performance, (2) ranking of contributors to nonperformance, (3) the probability of frequency concept for presenting results (see earlier discussion), (4) increased emphasis on evidence-based distribution functions (as opposed to assumed distributions such as Gaussian), and (5) the actual quantification of the risk of degraded performance.

As suggested above, the PRA thought process could very well be the primary vehicle for quantifying the safety and security risk of nuclear weapon systems and of other steps in the nuclear weapon functional life cycle such as the stockpile-to-target sequence and the issue of the aging stockpile and its effect on performance. The PRA framework is compatible with tracking multiple performance measures including safety, military compatibility, and logistics.

One final thought about how PRA might enhance the QMU process has to do with the changing of management mindsets about performance metrics. PRA has altered the thinking of nuclear power plant management about the importance of having multiple metrics for measuring risk and performance of complex systems. Maybe the weapons community has to do the same thing with its leadership. A single number for weapons reliability is not a confidence builder in understanding the performance characteristics of something as complicated as a nuclear weapon, where there is a need to expose the uncertainties in the reliability predictions.

REFERENCES

Garrick, B.J. 2008. *Quantifying and Controlling Catastrophic Risks,* Elsevier Press.
Jaynes, E.T. 2003. *Probability Theory; The Logic of Science,* Cambridge University Press.
Kaplan, S., and B.J. Garrick. 1981. On the Quantitative Definition of Risk, *Risk Analysis* 1(1): 11-27.

Appendix B

Committee Biographical Information

John F. Ahearne, Sigma Xi, the Scientific Research Society, *Co-Chair,* is the director of the Ethics Program for Sigma Xi and an adjunct scholar at Resources for the Future. His professional interests are reactor safety, energy issues, resource allocation, and public policy management. He has served as commissioner and chair of the U.S. Nuclear Regulatory Commission, system analyst for the White House Energy Office, Deputy Assistant Secretary of Energy, and Principal Deputy Assistant Secretary of Defense. Dr. Ahearne currently serves on the Department of Energy's Nuclear Energy Research Advisory Committee. In addition, Dr. Ahearne has been active in several National Research Council (NRC) committees examining issues in risk assessment. He is a fellow of the American Physical Society, the Society for Risk Analysis, the American Association for the Advancement of Science, and the American Academy of Arts and Sciences, and he is a member the American Nuclear Society and the National Academy of Engineering. Dr. Ahearne received his Ph.D. in physics from Princeton University.

Marvin Adams is a professor of nuclear engineering, the associate vice president for Research, and the director of the Institute for National Security Education and Research at Texas A&M University. Early in his career, Dr. Adams worked at Sequoyah Nuclear Plant (a TVA power plant) and its support office before entering graduate school at the University of Michigan, where he obtained his Ph.D. in nuclear engineering. There he began working on computational methods, focusing on problems involving particle transport. This effort continued after he became a code developer in the secondary-design division at Lawrence Livermore National Lab, and it has continued and broadened during 15 years on the faculty at Texas A&M University. Dr. Adams's contributions include improved discretization methods, theoretical analysis of the behavior of various methods in various limits, theory of iterative methods, and improved iterative methods. In recent years he has focused on efficient large-scale coupled-physics simulations and on assessing the predictive capability of such simulations. He led a project that developed and continues to improve the PDT code (3D massively parallel deterministic transport), and he directed Texas A&M's Center for Large-Scale Scientific Simulations. This center focuses on coupled-physics simulations with emphasis on quantitative assessment of predictive capability. Dr. Adams has served on panels and committees that review and advise the NNSA labs and DOE on matters including stockpile stewardship and the role of advanced scientific computing (ASC) in the weapons program.

John Cornwall received his A.B. from Harvard and his Ph.D. from the University of California, Berkeley. After postdoctoral positions at CalTech and the Institute for Advanced Study, he became a faculty member at UCLA, where he does research in elementary particle theory; later he became a professor of science and policy analysis at the Pardee RAND Graduate School in Santa Monica. He is the author of more than 130 refereed publications and contributions to books and coauthor of a roughly equal number of unpublished assessment and review reports in numerous technological areas. He has been a visiting professor at many institutions in the United States and abroad. For many years he was a consultant to the Space Sciences Laboratory of the Aerospace Corporation, where he did research on the magnetosphere and the aurora. He has served on the Defense Science Board and is a consultant to the Los Alamos and Livermore National Laboratories and to the Institute for Defense Analyses. He serves as chairman of the Defense and Nuclear Technology Review Committee of the Lawrence Livermore National Laboratory as well as chairman of the Predictive Science Panel reviewing strategic computing at Los Alamos and Livermore and is a member and for some years was vice chairman of JASON, advising the government on subjects such as ballistic missile defense, ultrasound technology, and the human genome project, among others. He has authored several works on, and testified to Congress concerning, ballistic missile defense, including as coauthor of the report *Countermeasures* of the Union of Concerned Scientists. He has been an adviser to, and lecturer in, the Public Policy and Nuclear Threats program of the Institute for Global Conflict and Cooperation at the University of California, San Diego. He is a fellow of the American Association for the Advancement of Science and the American Physical Society and a member of the New York Academy of Science and the American Geophysical Union.

Douglas Eardley is a professor of physics at the Kavli Institute for Theoretical Physics at the University of California, Santa Barbara. He was an associate professor of astronomy at Harvard University; an associate professor of physics and astronomy at Yale University; a research fellow in physics at the California Institute of Technology; a physicist in the T Division at Lawrence Livermore National Laboratory; and an assistant in the Caltech Infrared Astronomy Project. Dr. Eardley received an M.S. and a Ph.D. in physics from the University of California, Berkeley, and a B.S. in physics from Caltech. He was a member of the NRC Working Group on Related Areas of Science of the Astronomy Survey Committee; he has been a member of JASON since 1981; and he was a member of the NRC Committee on the Atmospheric Effects of Nuclear Explosions. From 1986 to 1989, he was on the editorial advisory board of the *Physical Review D*. Dr. Eardley's other memberships, responsibilities, and honors include these: member, Science Panel of the NRC Astronomy Survey Committee ("Bahcall Committee"); chair, External Advisory Board, Institute for Fundamental Theory, University of Florida at Gainesville; Physics Advisory Committee, Lawrence Livermore National Laboratory; plenary speaker, Texas Symposium on Relativistic Astrophysics; NASA Ultraviolet/Visible/Gravitational Program Review; Openness Advisory Panel, Secretary of Energy Advisory Board; coordinator, with R.D. Blandford and J.-P. Lasota, Program on Black Hole Astrophysics of the Kavli Institute for Theoretical Physics, which had three conferences; National Security Panel, University of California President's Council on the National Laboratories; chair, External Review Panel for the Radiation Effects Sciences Program, Sandia National Laboratories; and mission committee, Los Alamos National Security, Los Alamos National Laboratory. Dr. Eardley's research interests include general relativity: black holes, gravity waves, quantum gravity; theoretical astrophysics: X-ray sources, quasars, the active galactic nucleus, cosmology; mathematical physics: nonlinear partial differential equations; geometry; physics and society; national security; nuclear weapons; and arms control.

B. John Garrick (NAE) is an independent consultant who currently serves in a presidential appointment as chairman of the U.S. Nuclear Waste Technical Review Board. He has an active consulting practice in the development and application of the risk sciences to systems in the nuclear, space, chemical, and marine fields. Dr. Garrick has expertise in quantitative risk assessment and how risk assessment principles are applied as a fundamental part of engineering design. His research interests include the quantification and importance ranking of risks to humans and the environment to support societal decision making. He has served on numerous NRC committees, the most recent including the Committee on Assessment of Options for Extending the Life of the Hubble Space Telescope, the Committee on Combating Terrorism, and the Committee on End Points for Spent Nuclear Fuel and High-Level Radioactive Waste in Russia and the United States. He received the Society for Risk Analysis Distinguished Achievement Award and was appointed to the U.S. Nuclear Regulatory Commission's Advisory Committee on Nuclear Waste in 1994. Dr. Garrick was elected to the National Academy of Engineering in 1993. He has a Ph.D. in engineering and applied science from the University of California, Los Angeles.

Richard L. Garwin is an emeritus fellow at IBM's T.J. Watson Research Center. A member of the NAS, NAE, and IOM, his expertise is in experimental and computational physics and he has made contributions to nuclear weapons design, instruments and electronics for nuclear and low-temperature physics, computer elements and systems, superconducting devices, communications systems, behavior of solid helium, and detection of gravitational radiation. Dr. Garwin has served on numerous scientific boards and advisory committees, including the President's Science Advisory Committee from 1962 to 1965; the 1998 "Rumsfeld Commission" to assess the ballistic missile threat to the United States; the NRC Committee on the Effects of Nuclear Earth Penetrating Weapons and other Weapons; and the NRC Committee on Conventional Prompt Global Strike Capability. In addition, he has been an active member of the NRC Committee on International Security and Arms Control since 1980. He currently consults for Los Alamos National Laboratory and Sandia National Laboratories and is an active member of JASON. He has written extensively on nuclear weapons-related issues over the course of several decades, particularly on the question of maintaining the nuclear stockpile under the comprehensive test ban regime. Until August 2001, he chaired the State Department's Arms Control and Nonproliferation Advisory Board. He is a fellow of the American Physical Society and the American Academy of Arts and Sciences and a member of the American Philosophical Society.

Sydell P. Gold[1] retired as senior vice president at Science Applications International Corporation (SAIC), where she was responsible for SAIC's Defense Threat Reduction Agency's (DTRA's) business activities as DTRA account manager and for developing new business opportunities for

---

[1] Deceased, March 4, 2008.

SAIC. Previously, she was also the deputy sector manager, assisting the management of the Advanced Technology and Analysis Sector, a more than $350 million organization with over 2,000 employees specializing in systems design and engineering and computational and laboratory analysis and research. Prior to joining SAIC in 1992, Dr. Gold served for 10 years with the Office of the Assistant Secretary of the Air Force (Acquisition) as deputy assistant secretary (staff support and analysis) (acting) and as deputy to the assistant secretary. Before that, she served as a member of the professional staff at the National Security Council, as a technical staff member at Lawrence Livermore National Laboratory performing analyses of nuclear weapons and related security issues, and at Sandia National Laboratories utilizing applied mathematics and systems analyses for national security and nondefense issues. Dr. Gold received a B.A. from Barnard College of Columbia University, an M.S. from the University of New Mexico, and a Ph.D. in mathematics from the University of California, Berkeley.

Yogendra (Yogi) Gupta is Regents professor in the Department of Physics and Astronomy, and Director of the Institute for Shock Physics at Washington State University. He completed his B.Sc. and M.Sc. degrees at the Birla Institute of Technology and Science in Pilani, India. He completed his Ph.D. at Washington State University in 1972. After two years of postdoctoral work at Washington State University and Brown University, he worked for nearly 7 years at the Stanford Research Institute (now SRI International) as a physicist, senior physicist, and assistant director in the Poulter Laboratory. He joined Washington State University in September of 1981 as a faculty member and has been there since then. Dr. Gupta has been engaged in studies of condensed matter response to shock wave compression and nonlinear wave propagation since 1970, with a particular emphasis on the examination and understanding of microscopic processes. His background and training cover physics, materials science, and mechanics. With his graduate students and research associates he has been examining a broad range of multidisciplinary problems. Dr. Gupta has over 200 publications and over 200 invited and contributed presentations. Over the years, his research activities have been supported by the following agencies and organizations: NSF, ONR, AFOSR, ARO, DARPA, DOE, EPRI, NSWC, LANL, and LLNL. He is a fellow of the American Physical Society and the American Association for the Advancement of Science and a member of the New York Academy of Sciences. In 1995, he was chairman of the APS Topical Group on Shock Compression of Condensed Matter. He served as the first chairman of the Northwest Section of the APS upon its formation in 1998-1999. He has served, and serves, on many committees related to the national security mission of DOD and

DOE and is a member of the University of California's Science and Technology Panel. He received the American Physical Society's Shock Compression Science Award in 2001. In 2005, Dr. Gupta received Washington State University's Eminent Faculty Award, the highest faculty award bestowed by the university.

David Hammer is the J. Carlton Ward Professor of Nuclear Energy Engineering and professor of electrical and computer engineering at Cornell University. Dr. Hammer worked at the Naval Research Laboratory from 1969 to 1976, was a visiting associate professor (part time) at the University of Maryland from 1973 to 1976, and was an associate professor at UCLA in 1977; on three occasions, he was a visiting senior fellow at Imperial College, London. He has been a consultant to several corporations and government laboratories. Dr. Hammer has authored or coauthored about 110 articles that have appeared in refereed journals and about 60 that have been published in refereed conference proceedings. He also holds three patents. His research is supported by DOE's Office of Fusion Energy Science, by the National Nuclear Security Administration, and by Sandia National Laboratories, Albuquerque. Dr. Hammer is a fellow of the American Physical Society (APS), a fellow of the Institute of Electrical and Electronics Engineers, and a fellow of the American Association for the Advancement of Science. He has held several offices in the Division of Plasma Physics (DPP) of the APS, including chair of the DPP in 2004, and he is presently the division's representative to the APS Council. His current research interests and activities are centered on studies of pulsed-power-driven high-energy-density plasmas and their applications, with emphasis on wire-array z-pinches, and on plasma measurements by optical techniques.

Ted Hardebeck is currently vice president and director of science, technology, and strategy at Science Applications International Corporation. He previously served as associate director, concepts and assessments, and as the Commander's science and technology advisor at the U.S. Strategic Command (USSTRATCOM). Dr. Hardebeck's background is in nuclear weapons issues relating to network-centric military planning and analysis. At USSTRATCOM, he led a comprehensive examination of issues involving guidance, target base, weapons requirements, and stability, the results of which provided much of the foundation for the 1991 Presidential Nuclear Initiative. Dr. Hardebeck received a B.S. in mathematics and physics from Ball State University and an M.S. and a Ph.D. in mathematics from Case Western Reserve University.

John Kammerdiener is retired from Los Alamos National Laboratory. He received his B.S. from the United States Military Academy at West Point, an M.S. from the University of California at Davis/Livermore, and a Ph.D. from the University of California at Davis/Livermore. From 1961 to 1972, he served with the U.S. Army Corps of Engineers. He served in Vietnam as a major in the Army Rangers from 1966 to 1967. Later he was a research associate at Lawrence Livermore National Laboratory from 1968 to 1972 and was on the professional staff at Los Alamos National Laboratory from 1972 to 2001. In his 30-year career in nuclear weapons, he was the lead designer of many successfully tested nuclear devices, both fission triggers and thermonuclear secondaries, and he was a Los Alamos Laboratory fellow. From 2001 to the present, he has been a consultant to LANL, LLNL, and JASON. He was a contributing author of JASON studies on nuclear testing in 1995, 1996, 1998, and 2005.

Sallie Keller-McNulty is the dean of Rice University's George R. Brown School of Engineering. She previously headed the Statistical Sciences Group at LANL, where she led a wide range of R&D into model validation, reliability, defense analysis, and other topics. Before moving to Los Alamos, Dr. Keller-McNulty was professor and director of graduate studies at the Department of Statistics, Kansas State University, where she had been on the faculty since 1985. She spent 1994-1996 as a program officer in NSF's Division of Mathematical Sciences. Her ongoing areas of research focus on computational and graphical statistics applied to statistical databases, including complex data/model integration and related software and modeling techniques, and she is an expert in the area of data access. She has served on the Information Technology panel of the National Institute of Standards and Technology Board; the Committee on National Statistics' Panel on Research for Future Census Methods; the NRC Board on Mathematical Sciences and their Applications; the Committee on Applied and Theoretical Statistics (chair, 2000-2003); and the Computer Science and Telecommunications Board's Committee on Computing and Communications Research to Enable Better Use of Information Technology in Government. She is a National Associate of the National Academy of Sciences and fellow of the American Association for the Advancement of Science. She received her Ph.D. in statistics from Iowa State University. She is a fellow of the American Statistical Association (ASA) and has held several positions in ASA, including, currently, that of president. She is an associate editor of *Statistical Science* and has served as associate editor of the *Journal of Computational and Graphical Statistics* and the *Journal of the American Statistical Association*. She served on the executive committee of the National Institute of Statistical Sciences, on the executive committee of AAAS Section U, and chairs the Committee of Presidents of Statistical Societies, of which she is a former president.

Ernest J. Moniz is widely recognized for his work in theoretical nuclear physics and, more recently, in science and technology policy formulation. He joined the Massachusetts Institute of Technology faculty in 1973 and is currently the Cecil and Ida Green Professor of Physics and codirector of the Laboratory for Energy and the Environment. He previously served as head of the MIT Physics Department; as undersecretary of the U.S. Department of Energy; and as associate director for science in the Office of Science and Technology Policy. His current research-related activities include a foundation-sponsored project on the future of coal, work for LANL on security issues related to weapons of mass destruction, and service on a technical advisory board for EPRI. Dr. Moniz received a B.S. degree in physics from Boston College and a Ph.D. degree in theoretical physics from Stanford University. He has received honorary doctorates from the University of Athens, the University of Erlangen-Nuremburg, and Michigan State University. He is a fellow of the American Association for the Advancement of Science, the Humboldt Foundation, and the American Physical Society.

Michael Ortiz is the Dotty and Dick Hayman Professor of Aeronautics and Mechanical Engineering at the California Institute of Technology, where he has been since 1995. He leads the Solid Dynamics group of the ASCI/ASAP Center for the Simulation of the Dynamic Response of Materials. From 1984 to 1995 Professor Ortiz held a faculty position in the Division of Engineering at Brown University, where he carried out research activities in the mechanics of materials and computational solid mechanics. Dr. Ortiz received a B.S. in civil engineering from the Polytechnic University of Madrid, Spain, and M.S. and Ph.D. degrees in civil engineering from the University of California, Berkeley. He has been a Fulbright Scholar and a Sherman Fairchild Distinguished Scholar at Caltech and is a fellow and an elected member-at-large of the U.S. Association for Computational Mechanics, a Midwest and Southwest Mechanics Seminar Series Distinguished Speaker, and an Alexander von Humboldt Research Award winner. He has been editor of the *Journal of Engineering Mechanics* of ASCE and of the *Journal of Applied Mechanics*, associate editor of *Modeling and Simulation in Materials Science and Engineering*, and is presently associate editor of the *Journal for the Mechanics and Physics of Solids*, the *Archive for Rational Mechanics and Analysis* and the *Journal for Computational Mechanics*. Since 2002, Professor Ortiz has served on the Office of the President Science and Technology Panel for the University of California.

Jerry Paul has been named the first Distinguished Fellow on Energy Policy at the University of Tennessee's Howard Baker Center for Public Policy. He recently retired as the principal deputy administrator with the

National Nuclear Security Administration. In that position, he coordinated all activities of the NNSA at three national laboratories and five production facilities in the United States and foreign offices in Moscow, Vienna, Tokyo, and Beijing. Mr. Paul is a nuclear engineer and an attorney, and he was formerly a state representative in Florida. He served in the U.S. Merchant Marine and the U.S. Navy Reserve and has worked as a reactor engineer and power plant operator at fossil fuel and nuclear power plants. He served as a member of the U.S. Department of Energy Nuclear Energy Research Advisory Committee and as the Florida representative for both the Southern States Energy Board and the National Conference of Legislators Committee on Environmental and Natural Resources. Mr. Paul has a law degree from Stetson University, a bachelor's degree in marine engineering from the Merchant Marine Academy, and a post-baccalaureate degree in nuclear engineering from the University of Florida.

Robert Rosner, an internationally recognized astrophysicist, recently assumed the leadership of Argonne National Laboratory. Prior to that, he served as chief scientist at the institution since 2002. He was chairman of astronomy and astrophysics at the University of Chicago from 1991 to 1997 and since 1998 has been the university's William E. Wrather Distinguished Service Professor. He was the Rothschild Visiting Professor at the Newton Institute for Mathematical Sciences at Cambridge University in 2004. He was elected to the American Academy of Arts and Sciences in 2001 and is a Fellow of the American Physical Society. He holds a Ph.D. in physics from Harvard University and a B.S. in physics from Brandeis University. Most of Dr. Rosner's scientific work has been related to astrophysical fluid dynamics and plasma physics problems. Much of his current work involves developing new numerical simulation tools for modeling astrophysical phenomena, as well as validating these simulations using terrestrial laboratory experiments. He led the DOE-funded Center for Astrophysical Thermonuclear Flashes at Chicago from 1997 until 2002. Dr. Rosner's many scientific community services include current positions on the External Advisory Committee for the National Ignition Facility at Lawrence Livermore National Laboratory, the steering committee of the Interagency Task Force on High Energy Density Physics, the scientific advisory committees for the Max Planck Institute for Solar System Research, Lindau, Germany, and the Astrophysical Institute of Potsdam, Germany. As head of Argonne National Laboratory, Dr. Rosner is an opinion leader on several subjects, including energy research and development, accelerator science, computational science, and nanotechnology. He has been interviewed by CBS, National Public Radio, *E&E News*, and has been featured in *Inside Energy* and *Energy Daily* and locally in *Crain's Business Journal*, the *Chicago Tribune*, and the *Sun-Times*.

Robert Selden is currently a private consultant in defense science and research management. He retired in 1993 as an associate director at the Los Alamos National Laboratory. His career in the DOE national laboratories began at the Lawrence Livermore National Laboratory in the 1960s, when he was one of the two participants in the *N*th Country Experiment to design a nuclear explosive from unclassified information. After moving to Los Alamos in 1979, he served as the division leader of the Applied Theoretical Physics Division, as associate director for the Theoretical and Computational Physics Division, and as the first director of the Los Alamos Center for National Security Studies. Dr. Selden served as the chief scientist of the U.S. Air Force from 1988 to 1991 and received the Air Force Association's Theodore von Karman Award for outstanding contributions to defense science and technology. He has been a member of the Strategic Advisory Group to the commander of the United States Strategic Command since 1995. Since 2003 he has served as chairman of the Advisory Group's Stockpile Assessment Team, which is responsible for conducting a detailed annual review of the U.S. nuclear weapon stockpile. He also is currently a member of the Joint Advisory Committee on Nuclear Weapons Surety to the Secretaries of Defense and Energy. He was a member of the Air Force Scientific Advisory Board from 1984 to 2005. Dr. Selden received a B.A. degree from Pomona College and a Ph.D. in physics from the University of Wisconsin.

Appendix C

Glossary

Assessment

Assessment is a yearly procedure conducted to determine confidence in the original certification. It is much abbreviated compared to the certification.

Certification

Certification is the procedure required to assure the DOD that a warhead will operate within the military characteristics if the limits of the specified stockpile-to-target sequence are not violated. It is an elaborate procedure and does not need to be repeated often.

Hydrodynamic Tests (Hydrotests)

Hydrotests are non-nuclear experiments that study the behavior of a nuclear weapon primary from the ignition of the high explosive that drives the implosion to the point where the nuclear chain reaction would begin. These experiments are performed on inert primary pits that contain nonfissile material having properties similar to those of fissile plutonium. A variety of methods are used to monitor the behavior of the imploding inert pit metal. In one such method, pin domes are used (see below). Another method is to pass pulses of high-energy X rays through the imploding pit to record images of the process. The results of these hydrotests are used to validate models simulating the implosion of a weapon primary.

Input Parameters

Input parameters are the physical data that characterize the behavior of the materials used in a simulation. Examples are equations of state, opacity, and neutron cross sections. Input parameters can be selected for best fit to integral data such as that from underground nuclear tests. Input data are not knobs. Once selected for optimizing a baseline calculation, they remain fixed until the model is changed.

Knobs

Knobs are a resort to ad hoc normalization to integral data. There is no firm physics in a knob. If knobs are used in a baseline calculation, the knobs should remain unchanged from one calculation in a baseline suite of data to another. The degree to which knobs are used in a simulation weakens the ability of that simulation to model similar data.

Nuclear Explosive Package

The nuclear explosive package—also called the physics package—is the portion of a nuclear weapon that contains all of the components that generate the actual nuclear explosion; specifically, the fission primary—with its plutonium pit—and the thermonuclear secondary device.

Performance Gate

A performance gate is a range of acceptable values, defined by subsystem margins and uncertainties, for the performance of each of many subsystems in the chain of events occurring in a nuclear explosion. It is a range of values for some performance metric that must be achieved for success. These values are associated with the key components and operating characteristics of the weapon; their failure would severely compromise the overall performance of the weapon.

Performance gates vary in importance and type. All involve a performance threshold, expected performance variations, and performance margins. The nature of the margin depends on the gate. Examples include shape, timing, neutron fluence, criticality, temperature, yield, and functional mode.

The understanding of performance gates is incomplete.

Physical Inputs

Physical inputs define the problem to be simulated. Size, shape, thickness, mass, material, and density are examples. These are measurements and subject to random uncertainties.

Pin Dome Shots

One method for monitoring the behavior of an imploding pit is to mount a set of radial pins or wires of varying length in the shape of a dome at the center of a mock primary pit. During the implosion, the pins are short-circuited when the imploding pit metal comes in contact with the wire. The method produces a series of measurements giving the position of the implosion as a function of time.

Probability of Frequency

For repetitive risk scenarios for which the repetition frequency is uncertain but for which some evidence exists, the state of knowledge of that frequency value can be expressed by a probability distribution called a probability of frequency. See Appendix A for a more detailed discussion of this concept.

QMU

QMU is an important part of the process by which the results of weapons simulation computer models, experiments producing no nuclear yield, data from earlier underground nuclear tests, and expert judgment are brought to bear to assess the reliability of the existing weapons stockpile. The QMU process is analogous to the concept of engineering safety margins—i.e., the system is designed so that its operating margins are far enough from the failure thresholds to provide high confidence that the system will work reliably even though the magnitude and uncertainty of the margin for a particular performance metric may not be known with great precision.

Subcritical

Subcritical nuclear tests are tests of nuclear materials and components that do not produce a nuclear chain reaction—that is, they do not reach critical mass and therefore produce no nuclear yield. These tests are meant to produce data to help validate the simulation models and to be used in other aspects of the stockpile stewardship program.